TALES FROM AZAR'S ATTIC
A Look Inside A Broadcasting Career

by

RICK AZAR

BUFFALO
HERITAGE
UNLIMITED

Published by Buffalo Heritage Unlimited
Copyright © 2014 by Richard E. Carballada

Inquiries should be addressed to:
Buffalo Heritage Unlimited
266 Elmwood Avenue, Ste. 407
Buffalo, New York 14222
716-903-7155
info@BuffaloHeritage.com
www.BuffaloHeritage.com

ISBN 978-0-9788476-9-2 (softcover)
ISBN 978-0-9825745-0-8 (hardcover)
ISBN 978-0-9825745-1-5 (e-book)

Book design by Jon Guevara / 10zero6 Design

Front cover photo: Collection of Author

Printed in the United States of America

For My Family: Rick, Greg and Roseann, Christina, Michael, Claudia, David, and Jeff. And especially my wife of fifty-eight years, Edith ("Gaetana").

How does one put a value on family? One can't, because it's priceless. Some families have a tough time; that's not uncommon. When families are formed, it's mostly about "you, not me." Many times we lose our way, and it becomes "me first." That's when we get in trouble. My family is no different. Many ups, some downs. It comes with the territory. But it's a family that has stuck together through all of the difficult times and many felicitous times. Those are the times that make it all worth the trek. This book is not about them, it's for them, and for the many friends it has been our privilege to know. They are part of the family, too.

Favorite Quotes

"They'd better be pretty. You'll never hit the ball with an ugly club."

— Arnold Palmer, on selecting clubs

"His mother calls him Cassius, and so do I."

— Floyd Patterson, on Ali

"I never forget my friends."

— Chuck Knox

"Where would you rather be than right here, right now?"

— Marv Levy

"If you need me, I'll be there."

— Joe Crozier

"Tomorrow never comes. Do it today."

— Ramón Carballada (my father)

"To thine own self be true."

— Polonius (William Shakespeare)

"Darkness cannot drive out darkness: Only light can do that. Hate cannot drive out hate: Only love can do that."

— Dr. Martin Luther King Jr.

CONTENTS

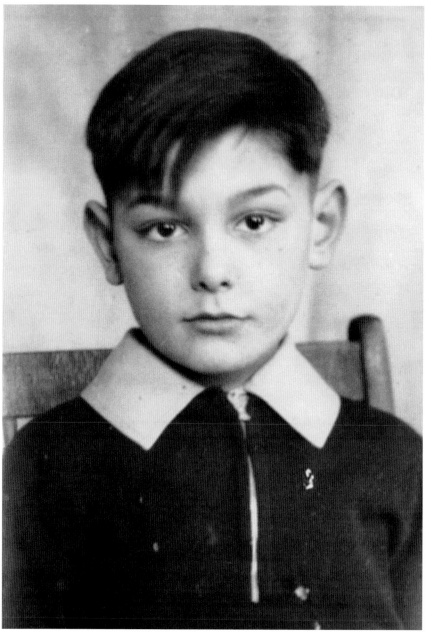

Fresh off the streets of Brooklyn, 1938.

1
My Story

My name is Ricardo Efrain Thomas Aquino Carballada de Babilón. That includes my baptismal name, confirmation name, father's surname, and mother's maiden name. You wouldn't think you'd need any more names than that, but I ended up taking on Azar as a stage name (more on that later). My father, Ramón, was from Spain; my mother, Esther, was from Peru, and they met and were married in Buffalo, New York. But that's another story.

I was born in Buffalo, but my family soon moved to New York City. The first days that lit up my mind were in Brooklyn. My mother owned a beauty shop at 285 Ninth Street, just north of Fourth Avenue. The shop was in a classic Brooklyn building with a ground-floor storefront and apartments above; we lived just above the shop on the second floor. It was a few blocks south of Prospect Park, which was where you started when explaining where you lived in Brooklyn: east, west, north, or south of Prospect. There, or Ebbets Field. My father was mostly out of work; we were in the middle of the Great Depression. He had all kinds of short-term jobs that in the long term served him well. He could fix almost anything and would accept most any challenge. He could change the spokes on a bicycle wheel or change the piston rings in an automobile; it didn't matter. Once, he built a bike from scraps after the one he bought new for me was stolen. He eventually became a millwright and an expert welder at Bethlehem Steel. My father was one of a kind.

So was my mother. She first came to this country as an au pair, traveling with the Perál family, who hailed from New York State. The journey ended in Buffalo. She too learned to do most anything, and she was an amazing cook, legendary in our family. Nearly all holiday meals were held in her small apartment on Ashland Avenue in Buffalo. The feasts she prepared served large gatherings of family, friends, neighbors, and informally adopted cousins. She, like my father, had minimal formal education, up to sixth grade perhaps. But she had a will that I have encountered in few people. Example: She was bound and determined that I learn to play the violin. Being a Spaniard, my father spoke up for the guitar, but my mother won. The violin eventually became one of the great joys of my life. Later she worked as a secretary at the International Institute in Buffalo and served as an unofficial welcoming committee for a multitude of Hispanic immigrants. My mother affected the lives of so many people. She was a giver of the first magnitude, tough as nails yet full of kindness.

Ramón Carballada, 1953. My father was a formidable man. He left Spain at the age of 16 after an argument with his father.

My mother, Esther Carballada, 1957. She came to Buffalo from Peru as a teenager and grew to be an enterprising woman.

Carballada family portrait, circa 1950.

My parents had three children, Sylvia, Ricardo, and Carlos. Sylvia was a beautiful little girl, who passed away from meningitis before she was three years old. My father never got over the loss. Sylvia had adored him, and he adored her. His grief was etched on his face until the day he died.

Carlos, my younger brother, was born in Brooklyn, but we moved back to Buffalo before his schooling began. I put in three years of school there at St. Thomas, and then it was St. Louis, St. Joe's Collegiate Institute, and Canisius College, all in Buffalo, for both of us. Carlitos, as we called him in his younger days, has had a successful career in business and education. He was president of several banks in Rochester, served as chancellor of the Board of Regents in New York State, and sat on various other boards. The list of his accomplishments in service to the communities of Western New York is endless. He even ended up as the mayor of Rochester, though only for a few months. The elected mayor, Bob Duffy, became lieutenant governor to Andrew Cuomo; his replacement resigned, and my brother, who worked in Duffy's administration as head of economic development, was there to save the day, albeit temporarily. When a new mayor was elected, Bob Duffy joked that the happiest man in the room was my brother. Not so, I think. Like my father, Carlos accepts most any challenge put before him. But that, too, is another story.

My parents didn't have any specific aspirations for my brother and me other than that we be educated and well-mannered. My mother might have liked me to become a concert violinist, but my life went in another direction. That's this story.

Taming the Ruffians

Some people don't have many nice things to say about the nuns they had as teachers back in the 1930s and '40s. The nuns I knew from those days were a tough bunch and rather high strung. But they had to be to take on the little ruffians who roamed around Brooklyn.

By the age of five or six, you'd already had your first street fight. It was a common occurrence to have some kid you didn't even know come straight up to you and forcefully inquire: "You wanna fight?" You learned to say "YEAH!" as loud as you could accompanied by your meanest look. Just that avoided many a brawl. If you were a pussycat, meekly saying "no," you were sure to walk home with a black eye or a split lip. It was a tough neighborhood. That's why the nuns gave us a whack once in a while. And you never complained about it, either. If you did, your parents had no sympathy. In their view, the nuns were right, and you got another whack from your dad — and maybe your mom — for even questioning the matter.

My family returned to Buffalo in January 1938 when I was nine. I found the nuns at St. Louis, in the city's Allentown neighborhood, to be a little calmer than those in New York City, but just as tough. I was starting the fourth grade, but struggled with the transition because I had skipped half a year. St. Thomas had been so crowded that they started a first grade in September and another in January. I was in the January group. So when I arrived at St. Louis, which did not have the same class calendar, I was pushed ahead into the second semester. It was a difficult adjustment at first, but my grades eventually improved.

Sister Margarite was the principal and seventh-grade teacher. Sister Gregory taught eighth grade. They were two of the brightest ladies ever. Sister Gregory was very proud of the fact that one of her students consistently earned a scholarship to one of the private parochial high schools in Buffalo. In fact, she was in the running to set a record. Because of me, my class broke the string. I was a good student, but I ranked tenth on the scholarship test, and only eight scholarships were awarded. Still, I was the only one of eight boys in the class to go to one of those schools – St. Joe's, which meant that my parents had to come up with a hundred bucks a year for the tuition. You read that correctly. I don't even want to guess what it costs today. Today, you might spend more than a hundred bucks on a date for dinner and a show. My parents struggled to pay that hundred dollars, and they did it for my brother, too. Same for Canisius College, where tuition was at least double, maybe triple what high school cost.

My father's primary ambition in life — my mother's too — was for my brother and me go to college. Unfortunately, my father died of an aneurysm on the ore docks at Bethlehem Steel at the age of 55. He never got to fully appreciate the benefits of the education he had made possible for my brother and me. Thankfully, my mother lived to the age of 100. I am forever grateful for their sacrifices.

Violin, My First Love

I don't think I was six years old yet, because I hadn't begun school. But I remember well how my love affair with something that has affected my life in so many ways came about. I'm talking about music, and in particular, the violin.

I was involved in a very serious game of stickball in the lot across the street from Puss 'N Boots, my mother's beauty shop, when a guy dressed like a salesman came up to me and, out of the blue, asked if I would like to learn to play the violin. Remember, this was the middle of the Great Depression. People took jobs they didn't know anything about and were happy to have them, so I'm not sure if this guy even knew what a violin sounded like. I didn't, but I pictured a stand-up bass — I have no idea why, except it also occurred to me that I was too small to play such a thing. "Naw," I said to him in my best Brooklynese, and the conversation ended.

My mother with Miss Phyllis and my Aunt Elena at the Puss 'N Boots Beauty Shop on 9th Street in Brooklyn in 1937, the birthplace of my love affair with classical music.

Fifteen or twenty minutes later I wandered into the salon, where business was slow, to find my mother; Tia Lela, my aunt and co-owner of the shop; and Miss Phyllis, one of the hairdressers, talking and smiling with the guy who had been trying to sell me on what I thought was a stand-up bass. The word violin came up again. It was a small instrument, three-quarters the size of a typical violin. Something you put under your chin with a bow to scrape along some strings.

Four broad smiles accompanied by convincing words urged me to try it. Play whenever I felt like it, they all agreed. No pressure. Sounded like any easy escape. Right off I felt I had total control. Wrong. The small print, which not one of the conspirators pointed out, said that I had to take a lesson every week and practice for an hour a day. To a Brooklyn kid more interested in stickball, this was a death sentence. I was trapped, with no way out.

Nothing sounds worse than a violin being played for the first time...and for some time thereafter. How my mother and father — well, maybe not my father; he was out looking for work most of the time — but how my mother could stand the awful sounds emanating from the upstairs apartment I'll never know. But the sounds eventually improved.

Our family, which now included my brother Carlos, soon departed Brooklyn. It was during this time that Hitler's army was invading every country in Europe, and people in the United States were getting nervous. The war machine was turned on. I was really too young to feel its impact, but for my father, it meant a chance at a steady job, which was the reason for the move. My godfather — I called him Padrino — who still lived in Buffalo, told my father to apply for work at Bethlehem Steel. No experience necessary. He did and was quickly hired.

A brief respite from lessons for a year or so followed as we adjusted to the move, but then I was enrolled in the First Settlement Music School on Elmwood Avenue. My teacher was Miss Dorothy Hebb, the school's director who also taught piano and voice. She

Settlement Music School recital, Buffalo, 1947.

got me from "Twinkle, Twinkle Little Star" to Saint-Saëns' Rondo Capriccioso and the Mendelssohn Violin Concerto. I loved it. First Settlement is now known as the Community Music School, and though it's located in larger quarters, it's still on Elmwood Avenue. I never studied there, but am proud to have served on its board for a time in later years.

Dorothy Hebb was a special teacher. She called the violin a fiddle, and for reasons I never understood, she called me Ichabod. She was not teaching me how to play country fiddle, but rather concert fiddle. And she insisted that I play to her expectations. If I showed up for a lesson unprepared, my parents found out about it. My punishment was to practice at the school on a Saturday morning under Miss Hebb's usually watchful eye. To a 13-year-old, however, Saturday is sacred, with hours of basketball to be played.

On one particular punishment Saturday, I showed up at 9 a.m., was assigned a third-floor room, and was left there to practice. For a few hours I practiced hard until my hands started getting tired. I was sure Miss Hebb was going to check up on me, but there was no sight of her or anyone else. Soon my mind wandered from the violin, thinking about the basketball game I was surely missing. By 2 p.m. I thought the world had forgotten about me.

A calm mother with her nervous son before his first Kleinhans Music Hall recital, 1950.

As it turned out, Miss Hebb definitely had. When I finally slinked down the stairs to find her at her desk, she cried, "Oh my God! Ichabod! I forgot all about you!"

I never had a bad lesson from her again and ended up studying the fiddle for sixteen years. Miss Hebb had such a great influence on my life that I once hoped I'd go to Juilliard, though I ultimately chose another direction.

Other Youthful Pursuits and College

While the violin was a big part of my life, sports and drama were others. I was not a great athlete, but I loved playing baseball, sandlot football, and especially basketball. On Saturdays I'd play hoops with my friends from nine in the morning until it was time for supper. My father thought organized football was too rough and banned it. (Interestingly, he loved hockey and would have been a fan of the Buffalo Sabres had he lived long enough to see them play.) There were many days when Miss Hebb wondered about my swollen knuckles and scraped fingernails.

Every kid I knew when I was growing up played baseball, or at least tried to. Our grammar school team wasn't very good, but we were out there trying, especially because we had a strong-armed pitcher known to all as "the Weeper." I have no idea why we called him that, and I can't remember his given name. But he struck out a lot of guys. And our team struck out plenty, too. But we played.

I tried out for the St. Joe's baseball team as a pitcher, but didn't make it. We had some great athletes on that team, including Paul "Skip" Hogan, Bucky Illig, Jackie Lyons, and Bill O'Conner. Still, I had a claim to fame. We were scheduled to play Nichols High School one Friday afternoon. Skip Hogan was set to pitch, but he forgot his glove. I still had mine in my locker and saved the day.

Skip used my glove that day to pitch a perfect game: no runs, no hits, no errors. I'm still trying to get my glove into the St. Joe's Sports Hall of Fame.

In my youth the CYO, or Catholic Youth Organization, was a major outlet for teenagers. Unlike today, Catholic churches and schools were located all over Buffalo. I was on the CYO's basketball team, debate team, and drama team, which every year put on a one-act-play contest. All had my attention. The debate team was my first taste of public speaking. The basketball team won few games, but the drama team was unbeaten three years in a row. Father Jim Cahill, assistant pastor of St. Louis Church and moderator of the St. Louis CYO, put all that together for us kids.

Sports, the violin, and the CYO dominated most of my high school life, but at Canisius College it was the Little Theater and the intercollegiate debate team. During those times, I had the privilege of studying with countless teachers who had a distinct effect on my life. That goes not only for the nuns in grammar school but also for the lay teachers and Christian Brothers who ran St. Joe's and the Jesuits at Canisius.

Dr. Charles Brady, who taught English at Canisius College, was so good at what he did that no one ever thought of cutting his class, not even the football players. That's how special he was.

He involved his students in discussing everything from books to authors to poetry, even venturing off into current and ancient cultures, history, political systems, geography, you name it. I consider him one of the smartest men I've ever known, not just because of his in-depth knowledge of those topics, but because he taught us the thought process and how to express ourselves properly, both orally and in writing.

In our senior year, Walter Barrett, a well-known local actor and English and drama teacher at the college, directed *Hamlet*. Many of my friends were in the production. Bill Conroy played Hamlet. He later became an FBI agent. J.B. Walsh played Polonious. He became a prominent Buffalo attorney. Max McCarthy was the gravedigger. He became a US congressman. I played Laertes, and that started something for me, as well.

During the summers in college, while my pals were sweating it out at cement plants or on factory floors, I was fortunate to get some replacement jobs in radio — first at WHLD in Niagara Falls, then at WUSJ in Lockport, and finally at WWOL in Lackawanna. This started in the summer before my freshman year at Canisius. Father Cahill had become a close friend of the family and a confidant of mine. He often had a seat at our dinner table. Over one such meal, as I was lamenting my future, trying to decide what to do with my life, he suggested that I try radio; he thought

While still in high school, I worked at WUSJ in Lockport. Here I am reading the news of the day.

my experience in theater would lend itself to broadcasting. Plus, he had an in: the director of our award-winning CYO plays was Nick Santasero, then manager of the Erlanger Theater in Buffalo. Nick was pals with the manager of WHLD. Not long after that fortuitous dinner, I auditioned at WHLD and got the job. Father Cahill became a life-long friend and presided over my marriage to Edith Centofanti. But more on that later.

Appearing in *Madwoman of Chaillot* with the Mark Twain Masquers,
Hartford, CT, 1951.

2
ON THE BOARDS

HARTFORD

After graduating from college in 1950 I was off to Hartford, Connecticut. A college professor of mine had given me a tip that the National Fire Insurance Company of Hartford was looking to break into the Latin American market, and, since my parents had seen to it that I spoke Spanish fluently, I got the job. I enjoyed my part-time radio jobs, but I had a steady girl at the time. If we were to become engaged, I needed a secure career; the job in Hartford seemed like a smart move, even if it wouldn't be as much fun as being on radio. I had to make a decision about what I wanted to do versus what I needed to do, and the insurance job won.

I was assigned to sales in the Latin American Department, which was run by a Spaniard from Galicia, the same province in Spain that my father came from. It got me off on the right foot. Because I knew no one in town except for my fellow workers and the lady who ran the rooming house where I lived, my bosses, who knew of my background in college, suggested I join a community theatrical group known as the Mark Twain Masquers. It was the beginning of a new direction for my life.

The Masquers were a talented group, all amateurs except for the director, Paul Neil DeSole, who ran a summer-stock repertory playhouse just south of Hartford and had been hired by the Masquers for a five-play season. Several members of the company went on to professional careers, including Ted Knight, who starred on the "Mary Tyler Moore Show" and also worked in Hollywood. Ed Begley Sr. had been an early supporter of the troupe, and Peter Falk got his start there shortly after my time with them. I played small parts in productions of *The Madwoman of Chaillot* and *Anna Lucasta*, among others. Troupe members did everything necessary for the production: set construction, lights, the works. It was a lot of fun.

Based on my work with the Masquers, DeSole cast me in Sidney Coe Howard's *The Silver Cord*, a production of his summer stock playhouse. Sure enough, Payton Price, a New York City theatrical director, saw me perform and suggested I should be in New York. He'd been working in New England on another summer stock production, stopped in Hartford occasionally because he was designing a theater for the town, and, as it turned out, we had mutual friends. Though whether true or not, he claimed to have given Kirk Douglas his professional name. Price planted another seed.

I'd been in Hartford for two years; a career in insurance was laid out for me. But my enthusiasm for a safe job had ebbed when it turned out that my girlfriend back home wasn't being so steady with me. Thoughts of an engagement were over, and thoughts of acting, which I'd had since my high school CYO days, occupied my mind. All it took was Price's remark to propel me. With $100 in savings — a nice sum in those days — I was off to the Big Apple to try to make it as an actor. I figured my savings was enough to keep me fed for a month or so. Luckily, my cousin Julio Valdivia ran a rooming house on State Street in Brooklyn — the same Brooklyn I remembered. He was Peruvian, the son of my mother's sister, Tia Lela, and his life demands a book of its own. But he gave me a place to live rent-free.

The Business of Acting

"Making the rounds" was a familiar phrase for actors, especially those without an agent. It meant going to "cattle calls," or open auditions, pounding on agents' office doors to leave a head shot and résumé, and getting together with other unemployed actors for coffee and dinner at Horn & Hardart's, a famous New York curiosity in those days, full of vending machines. Put some coins

PHOTO: JAMES HARGISS CONNELLY PHOTOGRAPHY / COLLECTION OF AUTHOR

My professional acting head shot.

into one of the countless slots, and out popped a sandwich or most anything else. You could buy fresh vegetables, fruit, dessert, whatever, for a nickel a serving, which provided many an actor with sustenance for months on end. In similar fast-food joints around town, most waiters and waitresses were actors; we would do almost anything to keep the dream alive.

I remember scoffing at anyone who would stoop to modeling. I thought of it as selling one's body, but not in the sense you're probably thinking. It just seemed a bit seedy, and anyway that wasn't why I was there. I was an actor, after all. But guess what? I stooped. I was down to my last buck. In the Help Wanted section of the *New York Times* that my cousin Julio bought I saw that L. Grief and Bros., a men's clothing manufacturer, was looking for a male model for its spring sales season.

First thing that Monday morning I was at L. Grief and Bros., on Broadway and 29th Street. The outer room was packed. I was last in line. There must have been twenty guys ahead of me. I'd bet most of them were actors. There wasn't a lot of talk. Like me, I suppose, no one wanted to let on that they really needed the job. One by one the applicants filed through a door at the end of the waiting room, each one coming out a few minutes later. My turn arrived. All I needed to do was try on a jacket from the spring collection. Apparently, they were looking for someone of average height and build, and somehow that jacket was meant for me. It fit perfectly. I got the job. What a relief! Six weeks of work with an option to come back for the fall season. Prayers do get answered.

That job led to several major turns in my life. The modeling income allowed me to take acting lessons at the Herbert Berghof Studio, which the actor and director co-owned with his wife, Uta Hagen, the German-born actress who first played Martha in *Who's Afraid of Virginia Woolf* on Broadway. Five dollars a class. Occasionally, because of Berghof and Hagen's other commitments, other well-known teachers substituted. One was Mira Rostova, Montgomery Clift's inner soul. It's been said that Clift wouldn't do anything without her permission. She was a stirring teacher who never questioned herself. I recall a scene study in which I played a gangster intruding on a man in his home. The actor I played against had his own ideas about how the scene should go. I had conviction in my role, but my partner kept distracting me. Later, Rostova counseled me: "Rick, when you gave your first lines, you had me completely, but then it was gone." She taught us to know exactly what we were doing with each line of script; about projecting and communicating meaning; and to do that consistently, line by line. It was an important lesson that would serve me well later in my broadcasting career.

The other turn was meeting Harold Shack, who would come to be my best friend. He was an apprentice salesman at L. Grief and Bros. Harold's sister, Lynn, was in the chorus line at the Copacabana. That connection opened the door to many a party begging to be crashed. Lynn was a church-going straight arrow. She and the other girls in the line were forever being invited to parties by nice guys and not-so-nice guys, and Harold and I were asked along just in case. Neither of us was a tough guy and, thankfully, we never had to pretend we were.

The adventures Harold and I had in a brief three years could fill another book. He was a fun-loving guy who later became successful in the clothing business. He had a tragic accident in the mid-'70s when I was already at Channel 7 in Buffalo. Lynn called from New York to tell me about it. I just happened to be leaving for New York the next day to do a Sabres-Rangers hockey game, so I was able to visit him. Tears streamed down my face when I saw him in a wheelchair. Both his legs had been amputated when he slipped on the platform while trying to catch the last train home from the city to Hollis, Long Island. In Harold's opinion, the consequences of the accident were never more than a minor inconvenience. He had a wonderful family to support him and lived for another twenty years after the accident, working until the day he died. I'll never forget him and to this day tell stories about him.

One story that doesn't involve him involves his sister, Lynn, who called to ask if I was going to be in Manhattan that afternoon and if we could meet for coffee. Done deal. While sipping coffee, she mentioned she'd been invited to a cocktail party at the Waldorf Astoria Towers that evening hosted by Hugh Bradford, an oilman from Texas. Lynn was a little skittish about going and thought it might be a good idea if I went along. I hesitated, then suggested she phone him with the story that she had run into an actor friend and would like to bring him along. Not a problem, he said.

We were the first to arrive, and evil thoughts about Hugh's intentions were erased after about ten minutes. The place was soon packed like an unopened jar of pickles. After an hour or so, Lynn had to leave for the first show at the Copa. My intention was to leave, too, but Hugh insisted that I stay and join him and several others for dinner, after which we would go to the Copa for the second show. Jimmy Durante was starring.

I resisted, knowing that I had only three dollars in my pocket. But Hugh wouldn't let me leave, and Lynn was no help, also encouraging me to stay. So off she went to the Copa and off I went with Hugh, one of his pals — a freeloader — and four young ladies.

For dinner, we ended up at the El Morocco, one of New York's swankiest restaurants. The cab cost me a dollar (the freeloader never made a move) and it was 25 cents to check my coat. I decided then and there that I would not eat. The freeloader didn't eat either, but he had an alcoholic beverage. I had a ginger ale. Hugh protested, but I claimed I'd eaten too many tidbits at the cocktail party. A paltry excuse, but I stuck to my guns.

Dinner over, Hugh proceeded to pick up the check, including gratuity. I laughed, because I wouldn't have been able to contribute to the tip either if I expected to have enough subway money to get home. Off to the Copa. Another buck for the cab and another quarter to check my coat. Fifty cents left. The group had now grown to about fifteen people, and Hugh had arranged for us to have stage-side seats right where all the entertainers passed by. I knew most of the girls in the line because of Lynn, and they all gave me the high sign as they passed. The guests were duly impressed. As I mentioned, Jimmy Durante was the headliner and needless to say he was a smash, being called back three or four times for a bow. On his last pass by our table, he stopped, threw his arm around my shoulder and asked, "How'd you like the show, kid?"

"You were never better," I said.

"Glad you liked it," he said.

Now everyone at the table was really impressed, and all I could think of was that fifty cents I had left in my pocket. True story.

WHERE DID AZAR COME FROM?

While I was looking for acting work in New York, there was a common line of questioning used by agents. It usually went something like this: "What have you done? Where have you worked? Stage work? Radio work? TV work?" And the clincher, "What was your name again?"

My first name, Rick, of course, came from Ricardo, but few in the industry in the early days knew how to pronounce my last name. Most talent agents offered the same solution: "Change it." It was common in those days for actors and others in the public eye to change their names. Hollywood was full of people with names completely unlike the ones their parents had given them. So was Broadway.

I never experienced any prejudice because of my ethnicity, but an ethnic last name with ten letters was perceived as an impediment. So I set out to find a new name for myself, a catchier one, but one that would also sound "real." I tried to think of something simple and easily remembered, but still in keeping with my Spanish heritage. I scoured a map of Spain and found the suffix "-azar" on many family and place names: Salazar, Solazar, Alcazar. And there it was. Four letters. Easy to remember, and most agents thought

With my brother, Carlos, at the 1974 WNED-TV auction. He joked that he changed his name from Azar to Carballada.

it was a good choice that went well with Rick.

My brother, a prominent businessman in Western New York, was often asked: "How come your brother's name is Azar?" His response: "I never liked Azar, so I changed mine to Carballada."

Today, few people in the entertainment industry change their names. The more ethnic the better. I like that. Now there are thousands of Carballada-types living in this country. Had I known that was going to happen, I never would have changed it.

BARTER THEATRE

While I was studying with Herbert Berghof, Barter Theatre auditions were held by the producer Robert Whitehead at the American National Theater and Academy on 57th Street. The Barter Theatre opened in 1933 and today is one of the longest-running professional theaters in the nation. It's located in Abingdon, Virginia. Whitehead started his career there in 1938, and by the time of my audition in 1953, he had become one of the most respected producers on Broadway. Back then, at least, big-name Broadway and Hollywood stars held court as the judges for New York auditions. The previous year it had been the Academy Award winner Fredric March, and the year we auditioned it was the writer and actress Cornelia Otis Skinner. I say "we" because a fellow student, an actress whose name I cannot recall, and I did a scene study from *The Rose Tattoo*. Since more than seven hundred actors were auditioning, each was allowed one minute, so we had two minutes to do part of the scene. We were the only ones to do that. The rest did monologues. Ten actors were picked — four men and six women. My partner and I were among the ten. One man and one woman went to Virginia; the others were offered jobs in a pageant touring the South that summer. One of the other guys was Martin Landau, whom I knew and who accepted the pageant offer. Disappointed that I didn't make the cut for The Barter, I passed. Needless to say, Landau had a very successful career in Hollywood.

Much to my surprise, a few days later I received a gracious letter from Miss Skinner. She was appearing in a one-woman show on Broadway called *Paris 90*. She said she would like to meet with me and told me to come backstage after one of her performances. All I had to do was present the letter to the usher or doorman, and I would be allowed in. I never did go. I had already seen the show.

To this day, I can't believe I was that stupid.

SUMMER STOCK

Summer stock productions still exist in this country, but not as many as there once were. I played in such productions while still in college and found them a great summer activity for young actors. They were also a means for professionals to keep their careers alive. Hollywood types were known to "take to the boards" so they could remember how to act on a stage.

I signed up for a stint in Barnsville, Pennsylvania, at a playhouse owned and operated by John Kenley, a well-known New York producer. Hundreds of actors — and that's not an exaggeration — famous and otherwise, had worked for him at one time or another. I was one of the "otherwise" and did it for the work and as a way to get my Equity card. Having an Equity card stamped

Appearing in *The Postman Always Rings Twice* in Barnsville, PA 1953.

you as a professional and was good for the ego. If you were an actor, you'd better have an ego, even if it didn't show. If you didn't think you were good, nobody else would either.

So there I was in Barnsville, doing bit parts in plays with people like the Hollywood actors Tom Neal and Barbara Payton. They were doing *The Postman Always Rings Twice*, in which I played a sailor. Those two were a hot commodity, in more ways than one. The gossip scribblers were having a field day with them, so all their shows were sellouts. Seems Payton was having an affair with Neal while still married to Franchot Tone, another big-deal actor who was from Niagara Falls. Tone and Neal were all over the papers after a one-round fight that resulted in a broken beak for Tone. Neal and Payton continued their relationship in Barnsville and in every other town where the play was booked. Despite all the attention, they were more than gracious to those they worked with, including me. The real story is sometimes less interesting then the manufactured one. Nevertheless, gossip fiends couldn't get enough. Some things don't change.

But back to John Kenley: He had a play in residence at the Schubert Theatre in Chicago called *Maid in the Ozarks*, a comedy with plenty of laughs, but it never had a chance for a Tony, or a Pulitzer, or any other literary prize. One of the actors was leaving and Kenley thought I would fit the part of Thad, a wacky kid. I was 24 years old and off to Chicago.

THE WINDY CITY

Chicago lived up to its name in every way imaginable. It is everything everyone has ever said or written about it, and its heart never stops beating. The arts abound. It has a great symphony orchestra, art galleries, and jazz joints that play all night. Top-notch theaters that seldom go dark. And don't forget the Cubs, the White Sox, the Bears, and the Blackhawks, along with Lake Michigan and that ethnic flavor that gives a city its soul. I felt at

As Thad in *Maid in the Ozarks*. Starving actors will take any part they can get.

home, because Buffalo, while not as big, has many of the same qualities. I went into rehearsal immediately, and a week later I hit the boards. *Maid in the Ozarks* played in Chicago through July and August 1953. We had a great cast, with a Chicago vaudeville veteran named Pinky Tracy and RKO actress Rusti Salmon in the lead roles.

Another play in residence that summer, *New Faces*, had a cast full of future stars: Paul Lynde, Robert Clary, Ron Graham, Alice Ghostley, Carol Lawrence, and Eartha Kitt, among others. Members of both casts hung out in the same joints after performances. We shared a lot of laughs. Miss Kitt and I were guests together on a late-night radio talk show hosted by Jack Eigen, who was a familiar voice to Chicagoans throughout the '50s and '60s, a time when entertainment talk shows were quite popular. In Eigen's case, he often broadcast live from the Chez Paree lounge in the Streeterville neighborhood, where we met him for his show. He was the acerbic type, but we charmed him. Or at least Eartha did. For me it was an early lesson on when to talk and when to keep your mouth shut. The whole Chicago experience made me feel as though my career in show business was on its way. Little did I know.

We took off on a four-month tour with stops in Kansas City, Missouri; and Terra Haute, Vincennes, and Anderson, Indiana.

Then to Canada — Toronto and Hamilton — and on to Buffalo. What a thrill for me to be back in my hometown. I had seen some theater greats perform at the Erlanger Theater, which, sadly, was later demolished. I'm happy to note, however, that theatrics are thriving in my beloved hometown, with many active live theaters, along with all the other arts, including the marvelous Buffalo Philharmonic Orchestra, which plays in Kleinhans Music Hall, one of the best performing venues in the country, if not the world. It's as acoustically perfect as it can be. Many of the world's great conductors have come to Buffalo specifically to perform in that building. I met several of them later in my trek through life. I still love going there. And of course, the Albright-Knox is one of the highest-ranked art galleries in the nation for modern and contemporary art.

Anyway, the show went from Buffalo to Pittsburgh, where the run ended. My next stop was New York, but the stay was short. By the middle of December 1953, I was headed back to Buffalo for the Christmas holidays. Before I left, I visited with friends and also stopped at the Deborah Coleman agency, which had taken me on. They had not completed the paperwork, so I guessed signing the papers could wait until I returned from a couple of weeks upstate. I didn't know it then, but my journey was about to go in another direction.

The girl in the yellow dress, 1953.

3
ON THE AIR

NIAGARA FALLS AND THE GIRL IN THE YELLOW DRESS

I had worked summers at several radio stations while I was in college. The last of them, WUSJ, wanted me to stay on, but that probably would have meant missing my senior year at Canisius, and that was not going to happen. While I was in Buffalo for the Christmas holidays, I ran into Eddie Joseph (everyone called him Eddie Joe), an announcer I had worked with in radio during my college days who was now the general manager at WHLD in Niagara Falls. The night we met he offered me a job that I had no intention of taking. I was going back to New York City to continue what I thought was my budding acting career.

Eddie promised a good wage and said they were in desperate need of help. I said I'd think it over and give him an answer in a day or two. But Eddie was persistent. My delaying tactic didn't work. He wanted an answer. I began to think that I could do both: take the job until the first of April, put a few bucks away, and then head back to New York City.

I never got there.

CHAPTER 3

I was invited to party at Luigi's, a restaurant in Niagara Falls. Mostly press and radio people attended the event, and there I ran into Del Monaco, a high school pal who was working at WJJL, the other Niagara Falls station. We had played fiddle together in the St. Joe's band. After catching up, he asked if I had any music contacts in New York City.

"One of the best," I said, thinking of Danny Koessler, an independent producer and talent manager who'd started out at RCA Victor records. "Why?" I asked.

"There's a really talented singer here," Del replied. "I think she has definite possibilities, and she needs some contacts in New York. She may be singing later. You should hear her. She's standing right over there."

He pointed to a dark-haired beauty in a yellow dress, and I immediately thought: That's the girl I'm going to marry. And I hadn't even met her yet.

Del was right about her talent. A few months later she went to New York City, auditioned with CBS for *The Arthur Godfrey Show,* and was accepted. She studied with musician, songwriter, and producer Jerry Bresler. She sang at No. 1 Fifth Avenue in a showcase for new talent. She had all this going for her, but decided to come back home to her family and eventually to marry me instead. Talk about getting lucky.

It would be two years before the wedding of Edith Rita Centofanti and Ricardo Efrain Carballada took place in Niagara Falls. Despite my certainty when I met her, several obstacles got in the way of actually marrying her: her boyfriends.

Edith was a strikingly beautiful woman, and a plethora of likely candidates vied for her hand. I was not one of them and didn't presume to be, despite my first impression. A few get-togethers over coffee to talk about her potential career as a singer morphed into casual dates that eventually included meeting her vast family.

She was the youngest of seven children in an Italian family; her parents were immigrants just like mine. Because of our shared background and interest in music, we became good friends. But our dating was casual until a pal of mine met her while on a double date and asked if it was okay for him to ask her out. A gong went off in my head. "NO!" I emphatically answered, suddenly realizing I needed to act on my initial impression. After that, it was a matter of her saying yes. To me.

Finally, she did. I'll let Edith tell that story: "Rick was always getting parking tickets. The glove compartment in his car was stuffed with them. I used to tease him about it. One evening he

She said "Yes."

came to pick me up for a dinner date, and when we got in the car, he told me that he had gotten another ticket. I was a little mad at him, because he promised he wouldn't get any more. He told me it was in the glove compartment and to look at it. Inside was a small box, with an engagement ring inside. I said yes on the spot."

RADIO DAYS WITH JOE AND AL

My stay at WHLD from 1954 to 1958 was eventful in many ways. The Age of the Disc Jockey was busting out all over the country, and radio was in the midst of big programming changes. The Buffalo-Niagara Falls market was a major player.

When radio first got started, the networks allowed the use of recordings for sound effects only; all programming — including the background music for plays and soap operas and other musical performances — was done live in the studios, and affiliates picked it up for local listeners over telephone lines. Popular musicians stamped their albums with the words: "Not Licensed for Radio Broadcast" in order to protect their exclusive network performance contracts. But in the 1940s, a court ruling allowed radio announcers to broadcast recordings they had purchased, and the disc jockey was born.

The basic formula at the time was a mix of all types of shows, from poetry readings to variety shows to a classical hour, and

Azar's Attic, my radio show on WHLD, was mixed in with syndicated shows of the day.

nationally syndicated shows by well-known entertainers like Guy King and Lucky Pierre were mixed in with the local programming. It was common to have four or five announcers on staff. But in the mid-to-late '50s local jocks became more popular as much of the audience for comedy, drama, and variety shows left radio in favor of television. Radio moved toward the news, talk, and music format still popular today, and one-hour music shows expanded to two or three hours.

Because of its powerful transmitter, it didn't take long for our competition, WKBW Radio, to rule the airwaves of Western New York and most of the East Coast. Nationally known personalities passed through its doors. Record promoters couldn't wait to get their acts played on KB. Many major jocks spent time at the station; it was a regular who's who: Joey Reynolds, Dick Biondi, Russ Syracuse, Jack Armstrong, Jungle Jay Nelson, Fred Klestine, Tom Shannon, Perry Allen, and Danny Neaverth (one of my favorites). These guys really drove the Age of the DJ into high gear, with a personality-driven approach to programming; they decided what they wanted to play and became like trusted friends to their loyal listeners. In the '50s and '60s, radio was a totally different animal than the one you hear today. Now it's all preprogrammed. Back then it had style.

I made some new friends and rekindled old friendships during my second tour of duty at WHLD. One new pal was Al McCoy, who hailed from Iowa. Al had a mid-morning show, playing the piano live on air as well as spinning records, and he even sang once in a while. I had a show called *Azar's Attic*, playing big orchestral arrangements plus the hits of the day. Lucky Pierre ended up coming to Niagara Falls; he followed me, and later a jazz show was hosted by my colleague Joe Rico.

Al and I hung out with Joe as much as we could. He was a big-time impresario known to every jazz musician in the country. As a promoter, he brought the famous Jazz at the Philharmonic series to Buffalo many times and also booked the Newport Jazz Festival here for three years in the 1960s. He booked acts into a jazz joint called the Copa Casino, located on Main Street just north of Allen. Al and I spent many an evening enjoying the music there and meeting many of the world's great musicians and singers. Name one, and he or she probably played the Copa. Joe also booked the big bands for concerts — from Duke Ellington to Count Basie to Stan Kenton, all of them. Jazz greats too, like Dave Brubeck, Erroll Garner, Oscar Peterson, Gerry Mulligan. His list of the best musicians to play in Buffalo would fill ten pages of this book. Many of them dedicated songs to Joe Rico, he was so well respected.

A couple of quick stories....

It was the mid-1950s, and one August night Ellington was playing at the grand Hotel Niagara. In those days, Niagara Falls and Buffalo were regular stops for the top touring acts, since the region's population was at its peak. Not many patrons of the Hotel Niagara got to sleep early that night. People were dancing all over the mezzanine and lobby, and the band was at its best.

After the concert, Joe, Duke, and I went around the corner, hoping to find a spot for a nightcap with a few other friends. Even then, Niagara Falls didn't swing much past 1 a.m. A coffee shop had to do. Duke sat at the head of a table of eight. I was at his left; Joe at his right. The waitress came by, and Duke asked for some hard libation. The waitress, who had no idea it was Duke Ellington, said, "Sorry, we don't serve any." Without missing a beat, Duke turned and put his hand on my arm. "Son," he said, "you know where the tour bus is?" I nodded. "Go to the bus," he continued, "tell the driver I sent you. On the shelf above the seat behind the driver you'll find a brown paper bag. Bring it." Duke spiked his coffee that morning.

Another adventure had us taking in Dizzy Gillespie and his group one night at the Copa. During a break he asked if anyone in the audience played chess — I kid you not. I looked around and no one moved, so I said, "Me."

Like a magician, Dizzy pulled a chess board out of nowhere, motioned me to come up to the stage, and we had a game right then and there, much to the audience's astonishment and mine, too. It would be the first of several games Dizzy and I would play. Once, he even showed up at Joe's house, board in hand, knowing I'd be there. I reminded him of this many years later while he was booked at the Statler. He remembered, but confessed he hadn't come equipped. No game that night.

Another time, Dizzy showed up at the Copa after a Jazz at the Philharmonic concert. Al and I were there. Dizzy wanted to know if Miles Davis was there. One of us said, "No, why do you ask?"

Dizzy said he could have sworn Miles had been booked for a one-nighter at a jazz joint in Buffalo. He assumed it was the Copa. The three of us jumped into Al's car, and after looking into a couple of other possibilities, ended up at the Club Zanzibar, a little joint on Buffalo's East Side. Sure enough, there was Miles playing with a couple of locals. The place was about a third full, if that.

After his set, he came over to our table. Al and I were beside ourselves. Here we were with two of the greatest jazz trumpeters who ever lived. Miles and Dizzy were the best of friends, but you'd never have guessed it. Miles was the complete opposite of Dizzy. He greeted Dizzy as if he'd seen him a couple of hours before. Dizzy introduced us. We got a couple of grunts. The conversation was strictly between Dizzy and Miles. Al and I were too excited to care. After Miles went back to the bandstand Dizzy said, "Don't mind him. He's the moody type. Once in New York I went to his apartment. He opened the door, saw me, and slammed the door without saying a word. He's like that."

After marrying a Niagara Falls girl, Al took off for Phoenix and got a job as the voice of the Phoenix Suns NBA basketball team. He recently retired after serving many years and making a name for himself in the world of sports broadcasting. Just goes to show there's nothing like having a background in music, piano playing, singing, and disc jockeying to land you a job as a sportscaster. It happens all the time.

Joe Rico left Western New York for Miami and took the town by storm, doing the radio gig bringing the best of the best in the jazz world to south Florida. He is mostly retired now, playing tennis and living in Buffalo with his wife, Sharon. We visit each other all the time, and he remains one of my dearest friends.

STAFF ANNOUNCER 101

The first television station in Buffalo was Channel 4. Now known as WIVB and owned by LIN Media, it went on the air in 1948 as WBEN-TV, an extension of WBEN Radio — itself an extension of the *Buffalo Evening News*. It operated out of the

Hotel Statler, and every announcer in town wanted to work there. WBUF and WBES didn't come along until five years later, in 1953, and WGR, Channel 2 (now known as WGRZ) arrived in 1954.

Back then there were two kinds of television stations: UHF and VHF. The difference between UHF and VHF is too complicated to explain here — it has to do with megahertz and gigahertz, and it's all irrelevant anyway since the advent of cable and now the Internet. The point is, you needed a converter box to watch UHF stations, which severely limited their audience. WBUF and WBES were UHF stations.

In 1955, WBUF was sold to NBC. After winning an audition, that's where I got my first job as a TV announcer. Other staff members included Dave Thomas, Roger Lund, Joe Mendelson, Mac McGarry, and Jack Begon. Dave was from Buffalo and, like me, had changed his name, in his case from Boreanaz to Thomas. He started his radio career in Syracuse. We became fast friends. Roger Lund landed his first broadcasting job in radio while still in high school, so we had something in common as well. Mac McGarry was an experienced NBC announcer from Washington, D.C., and Jack Begon was a newspaper guy and former foreign correspondent. NBC sent him to Buffalo to gain TV experience. We all did all kinds of programming and had a great time doing it.

Saturday mornings were devoted to kids' shows. I had one called *Captain Smokey*. I dressed in regulation firefighter equipment and shared the stage with a sweet Dalmatian dog. I think it lasted a whole month, maybe two. Mac was the host of a morning kids' boxing show complete with a ring and boxers ranging in age from six to seven. Their gloves were so big you couldn't see their faces. Mac would introduce them giving their age and weight: "NOW HERE'S TIMMY STEVENS, SEVEN YEARS OLD AND WEIGHING FIFTY POUNDS."

For some reason, one morning Mac delivered the line for one of his usual guests as "FIFTY YEARS OLD AND WEIGHING SEVEN POUNDS." Really, really funny when you picture it. I had my own bloopers, of course. This was TV in its infancy. Announcers sat in booths with a microphone and little else, and everything was done "live," including station breaks.

Someone had to be in that booth every day from 6 a.m. until 1 a.m., when the station signed off the air. Station breaks — for station identification — occurred every thirty minutes. I was on booth duty one night watching *The Steve Allen Show*, tasked with signing off the station, which included reading a voice-over promo for the next day's newscasts while a film ran showing generic news footage with appropriate background music.

As Captain Smokey for WBUF TV. I think this show lasted about a week.

The script read: "THE EVENTS OF TOMORROW MAY DETERMINE WHETHER WE LIVE IN PEACE OR IN WAR."

I had done this announcement many times. But that night it came out, "THE EVENTS OF TOMORROW MAY DETERMINE WHETHER WE LIVE IN PISS OR IN WAR."

I thought my short career in TV was over.

Two things saved me. First, it was 1 a.m. and the only one in the building with me was an engineer who was having a good laugh at my expense. Second, as a UHF station, we didn't have many viewers anyway.

For a while NBC was on a quest to make UHF-TV a success, but the numbers never added up. Not enough converters were sold to make it profitable. So, in 1958, they discontinued operations and I was out of a job. By then, there were two children in the Carballada household.

I learned of an opening at a Denver station owned by Bob Hope. Yes, that Bob Hope. I wish I had a story to tell about him, but we never met. Denver then was a city just beginning to stir after languishing as a cow town for a long time. The people at the station were great. I passed their audition, and they offered me

A promotional shot for my weather show on WBUF TV, NBC's UHF
station, which folded in 1958.

a job. Meanwhile, waiting for me was an invitation to go to New York City to audition for NBC radio.

Denver would have been a big move. While I was considering the possibility, I realized what it meant to be an Easterner. I had grown up in cities and I was used to an urban landscape with access to all its benefits. To me, Denver was the middle of nowhere, nothing but the horizon to the east and the ominous-looking Rockies to the west. Though I told the bosses there that I had to talk things over with my wife before committing to the job, I guess I had already made up my mind. I turned down the Denver job, and I took the audition with NBC in New York City, where I was offered and accepted the job of staff announcer. I started a few days later. Because in those days NBC worked on twelve-week renewable contracts, Edith stayed in Buffalo for my first few months at the station, and I lived in a hotel near the United Nations.

While I was there, the Reverend Clinton "Doc" Churchill, an evangelical preacher, Doctor of Divinity, and owner of WKBW radio, opened a third VHF station in Buffalo. Out of the blue I got a call from a guy named Labe Mel, who was working for Churchill as program director at the new station. I didn't know him, but somehow he had heard of me, and he tracked me down in New York. Three months after I had taken the job with NBC,

Mel offered me a position as an announcer on the new TV station in Buffalo.

Dilemma time.

Edith and I had been talking about moving to New York City, but to make the move I needed a contract longer than three months. I asked the powers that be at NBC for at least a year's commitment, but was told they couldn't do that, so I gave them two weeks notice. They couldn't believe I would do such a thing, reminding me of how many people were waiting for an opportunity with a national radio network. But I was not ready to risk my family's security. I went to work for Doc Churchill and signed WKBW-TV, Channel 7, on the air for the first time on Sunday, November 30, 1958.

Two weeks later, NBC called asking me to come back. My answer was no, and I have never regretted that decision. An unbelievable ride had just begun.

BROUGHT TO YOU BY CAP CITIES

I was the first on board at Channel 7, but I won't go into any long dissertation about those early days under Churchill's ownership. Needless to say, the birth of another Buffalo TV station was exciting, but after the initial curiosity, the only ones watching us

PHOTO: COURTESY WKBW-TV

Covering the 1960 presidential election with fellow WKBW TV newsman, Hal Youngblood.

were...us. WBEN and WGR, with more experienced staff, had secured much of the local TV advertising and viewing market.

Our young group eventually learned the ropes, but it took a big change to really set us on a successful path. After the station's third year, Churchill was allowed to sell and sell he did, to Capital Cities Broadcasting. Clint Churchill, Doc's son, bought a radio station in San Francisco, and Doc retired out West.

Cap Cities' success story is legendary. It all started when the American travel and adventure writer Lowell Thomas and a pal of his, Frank Smith, bought control of Hudson Valley Broadcasting in 1954. After the company merged with Durham Broadcasting Enterprises in 1957, it really blossomed, making several purchases in the late 1950s and early '60s. One of the stations it bought was WKBW-TV in Buffalo.

It was a young firm full of eager and talented office and sales personnel. One of those young bucks was Bob King, the first of an extraordinary list of engaging general managers, each of whom had a hand in the development and success of Channel 7. The radio station was already number one in the market, with a bunch of wild and wacky disc jockeys doing their thing and newscasts called "Pulse Beat News" that weren't quiet and sleepy like most newscasts in those days. In 1964, King brought a guy named Irv Weinstein from radio to the TV station. In 1965, he swiped Tom Jolls from Channel 4, and the rest is broadcast history.

Larry Pollack followed Bob King as GM, and after Larry came Phil Bueth. Each, especially Bueth, contributed to the success of Irv, Rick, and Tom. The station did promotions and special ads that involved us; Bueth really knew how to leverage our personalities and the rapport among us. The ads were inventive and clever, and raised our visibility in the community. The viewers rewarded us by making us number one in ratings year after year through the '70s and '80s, but we didn't pay much

The Channel 7 team. From left: me, Channel 7 GM Bob King, Steve Zappia, Bill Gregory, Art Stofko. Bob thought we could win the American Bowling Congress championship. We didn't. A rare mistake on his part.

attention to that. We felt like we were just doing our jobs. Such success was not limited to Channel 7; with good, smart people running them, other Cap Cities-owned stations were generally number one in their markets, too.

By the mid 1980s, the company had expanded into larger markets and was negotiating to buy an ABC-owned and -operated station. ABC countered, suggesting that Cap Cities instead buy the entire network. If so, it would be a case of the little fish swallowing the whale with the help of Warren Buffett, who,

PHOTO: WKBW TV

Here I am interviewing 1960's teen-idol sensation Bobby Rydell on
Buffalo Bandstand.

OPEN: COURTESY WKBW TV

In the early days at Channel 7, I did a lot of things, including the weather.

among other successful enterprises, owned the *Buffalo News*.

However, Buffett was informed by Federal Communications Commissioner Thomas Murphy that his financial participation in such a deal would require him to sell the *News* because at the time an FCC rule prohibited companies from owning more than one communications arm in any one market. Sadly, this rule was later changed.

In response to the FCC mandate, I imagine Buffett politely told Cap Cities executives, "I'm keeping the *News*, so you'll have to sell KB-TV."

To ensure the deal with ABC and maintain Buffett's stake, Cap Cities sold WKBW-TV to Queen City Broadcasting, and the Cap Cities era in Buffalo came to a close.

"Buffalo Bandstand"

During the early days at Channel 7, I did a stint as host of *Buffalo Bandstand*. Every town in the country had its own *American Bandstand* copycat, and Buffalo was no exception. Rock and roll was "in," as the saying went. I was still listening to and playing Count Basie, Duke Ellington, and Woody Herman — but not on that show.

Once I played "Intermission Riff" by Stan Kenton during a "guess that tune" segment of the show. But management said: "No more of that stuff; rock and roll only." They finally got smart and turned the show over to the jocks from the radio station, but not before I got the chance to guest-host the national show in Philadelphia when Dick Clark was on vacation. It sounds more impressive than it was; everything was produced in advance, so there was no way to sneak in a favorite big-band tune. But still, there I was on national TV hosting one of the hottest shows of the era.

I enjoyed doing *Buffalo Bandstand*, but it was in better hands with a disc jockey. They were up to speed on the current pop-music scene. My departure allowed Tom Shannon to get his shot on TV.

In those early years, we were all considered staff announcers, and our roles were constantly changing. In addition to my Buffalo Bandstand duties, I was doing the weather, sometimes the news, and occasionally sports. For a short time, I was doing the news and sports while Dave Thomas handled the weather. Later, Bill Gregory came in as the news guy, and Stan Barron did sports. I settled into the weather while Dave went on to do some wonderfully inventive morning programming. At one point, I

this
is
the
team
to
watch
for...
News,
Sports and
Weather!

RICK
AZAR
NEWS
SPORTS

DAVE
THOMAS
WEATHER

7:15 · 7:30 P.M.
11:00 · 11:15 P.M.

For the Best in News, Sports and Weather... **BETTER DIAL 7**

Before the days of Irv, Rick and Tom, Dave Thomas and I shared
duties at Channel 7.

was asked to become the news director. In order to be effective in that role, I felt I needed to be there early each day. But the job also I meant I needed to stay late to do the 11 o'clock show. I had a young family; I didn't want to be gone all day and night. When sports director Stan Barron left to go to WBEN, I was offered that job and I jumped at the chance.

IRV AND TOM

After writing the names of Irv and Tom in that subtitle, I sat for days trying to figure out what to write next. The flood of ideas never stopped long enough for me to hit the keys. It made me appreciate even more the effort former WBEN news director Steve Cichon undertook in writing his book, *Irv! Buffalo's Anchorman: The Story of Irv, Rick and Tom*, a work born of passion about three men he really didn't know well. Oh, he knew us from television, and we spoke often enough, but he didn't have the benefit of a lot of interviews. Clearly, it was something he had to write, and I know I speak for Irv and Tom in expressing how much we cherish what he did.

I have no idea how many newscasts the three of us did after Bob King put us together. It got to the point where we took everything for granted. We never rehearsed anything. All the small talk was spontaneous. Irv was great at that, and Tom and I fell right into it.

This camaraderie was mostly experienced in the workplace.

The Irv, Rick and Tom team on the air.

Although we went to an occasional movie or play together, we generally didn't socialize much. We attended the weddings of each other's children, and we always found time to catch up on what our families were doing.

Irv and I had an "unscheduled" meeting almost every Monday, and we always found a way to connect when we were off the air. Tom had a workstation, but not an office, so after he finished his work on the weather, he would hang out in either my office or Irv's. We would talk and joke a bit, but we mainly focused on our jobs. Tom and I often ate dinner together at Jenny's, a local greasy spoon on Niagara Street near the Channel 7 studios, which had relocated from its original home on Main Street to where it is now in the heart of downtown Buffalo. We invited Irv to go to Jenny's with us, but no one could get Irv to go anywhere but Chef's, the famous Italian restaurant at the corner of Seneca and Chicago, where they actually named a dish after him. We had our twenty-fifth anniversary retirement reunion there.

I've often thought about a different circumstance, but cannot imagine anything better than what Irv, Tom, and I had. It could never have been planned. Fate does play a huge role in all our lives. Sometimes it doesn't turn out to our pleasure. Sometimes we are so fortunate that we don't even notice when the situation has changed. Irv and Tom are the dearest friends a man could ever have. Irv always says we're more like brothers with different mothers and fathers. We were all blessed.

PHOTO: COURTESY WKBW- TV

Irv and Tom are the dearest friends a man could have.

Sports journalists often wish they could have been athletes.

4
Do Not Adjust Your Set

It was a Monday in June 1975. ABC was very involved in championship golf at the time, and one of their scheduled tournaments was the US Open, which was being held at the number three course at the Medinah Country Club in Medinah, Illinois. All the big names of the day — Nicklaus, Palmer, Watson, Floyd, Player, Trevino — were there at the start. But not at the end.

Leading were Lou Graham and John Mahaffey. Nicklaus was two shots behind; Palmer trailed by three. Graham and Mahaffy finished their Sunday round tied after seventy-two holes, necessitating an eighteen-hole playoff on Monday. ABC, our affiliate, would begin telecasting the playoff around 3 p.m. I went back to the control room to remind our engineers and producers to tape the proceedings, so I could use highlights on the 11 o'clock sportscast.

All set, I thought.

Back in my cubbyhole of an office I turned on my television expecting to see the US Open final. What came up was a rerun of Mike Douglas's afternoon variety show. I ran back to the control room in a panic. They were taping all right, but the tournament was not being aired. By this time the phones were ringing off the hooks, and our receptionist was going crazy trying to answer irate sports fans demanding to know why the station wasn't showing the playoff round. I raced to the program manager's office only to learn he was in the general manager's office. Pacing back and forth I waited outside as my temperature rose like kneaded bread dough. Finally, I burst in unannounced, screaming: "Whose bright idea was it to replace the final of the US Open with a rerun of Mike Douglas? The phones are ringing like crazy! My credibility is in the trash. The phones haven't stopped!"

My face must have been purple. Calmly, Mr. Pollack, the GM, suggested I step out of the office and rethink this. With my veins still bulging and my voice at its highest pitch, I said: "I have already 'rethunk' it!" and stormed out.

The phones continued ringing. The receptionist was being berated unmercifully and was near tears.

The US Open is the mother of all golf tournaments, just as

the Kentucky Derby is the mother of all horse races. At World Series time, everybody is a baseball fan. It's like the Super Bowl, the World Cup, Wimbledon, the Masters, the Stanley Cup, the NCAA Final Four — when a championship is being contested, everyone is interested. My bosses insisted no one would care because none of the big names like Palmer, Nicklaus or Trevino were in the final. WRONG.

I knew I would have to apologize on the 6 o'clock news and again at 11 o'clock for the mix-up. I had a 6:15 p.m. sportscast to prepare, and time was running short. What to do? I decided to make it known that it was not the decision of the sports department to carry Mike Douglas. The tournament was still in progress, so on the early sportscast all I could do was relay who was in front and by how much. It was a difficult moment, dripping with apologies. Meanwhile, the irate calls were still pouring in and didn't let up until 10 p.m. On the 11 p.m. newscast I ran highlights from the taping. Lou Graham had beaten Mahaffey in a nerve-racking final, 71 to 73. I decided to take my apologies a step further and did a blistering editorial that unashamedly blamed the programming department for its flagrant television sin. Ready to accept the consequences, I absolved myself with three Hail Marys and expected those to be the last words I would utter on Channel 7.

The next morning I didn't get the phone call I was dreading, so I decided I might as well go to work. When I arrived, Larry Pollack told me he thought the editorial was great. I never heard another word about it. Fourteen years later I retired, after thirty years at the station. In the meantime, Walter Liss, the program manager who had favored showing Mike Douglas over the US Open, had become a golf addict. Go figure.

Commentary

The *Merriam-Webster Dictionary* defines "commentary" in part as a "systematic series of comments."

That definition, of course, forces you to look up "comment":
1. An expression of opinion.
2. An explanatory, illustrative, or critical note of observation.

If you ever read the editorial section of a newspaper, you are reading commentary. It's in a totally separate section of the paper, not to be confused with the rest of the stories that are factual, or at least, attempt to be factual.

In my day the same was true in television. Commentaries were normally left for the end of the broadcast and had to be identified as such. Thus, there was a clear signal to the audience that what they were about to hear was opinion.

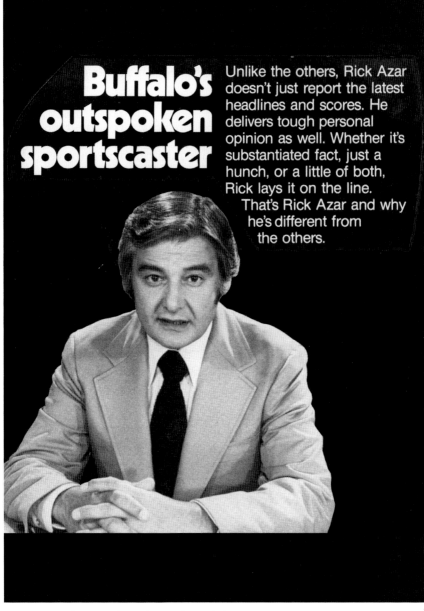

Buffalo's outspoken sportscaster

Unlike the others, Rick Azar doesn't just report the latest headlines and scores. He delivers tough personal opinion as well. Whether it's substantiated fact, just a hunch, or a little of both, Rick lays it on the line.

That's Rick Azar and why he's different from the others.

As sports director for Channel 7, I did a commentary from time to time.

I don't recall exactly when I first stuck my foot in my mouth to offer my opinion on a subject. Perhaps in the early 1970s, when community leaders were deciding whether a new stadium needed to be built to replace War Memorial Stadium. Originally called Civic Stadium, War Memorial had been built in the 1930s by FDR's Works Progress Administration. It was renamed when the AFL Bills began playing there in 1960, although no one ever called it War Memorial Stadium. Everyone called it the Rockpile.

By the time of the new-stadium discussions, the Bills had joined the NFL. If the team were to be successful, it needed to compete in a modern facility, but there was disagreement on where to locate it. The then *Buffalo Evening News* (now the *Buffalo News*) and the now defunct *Courier-Express* used their editorial pages to express competing views on the best location.

From a reporting point of view, all the debate made for an exciting time. In addition to the print editorials, reporters weighed in with their opinions on the best site. I dove into the debate with glee. As the story unfolded, I ran a series of commentaries emphasizing the importance of constructing a new stadium, feeling strongly that the differing opinions on location distracted from the overriding need to get the project underway. Buffalo needed a major-league stadium to retain its major-league franchise. The stadium did get built, of course, and some controversy lingers still about how that unfolded, which is a story I'll tell later. But at the time I felt there was a big risk that the project would not happen at all.

From then on the word "Commentary" appeared below my mug with some regularity — always at the end of my show. My bosses wanted me to do the editorials weekly, but I believed that would risk commenting just to comment. I didn't want to manufacture controversy, but when a matter came up that I felt needed to be discussed, and I had a strong opinion, I felt obliged to use my platform to express it.

The Media

The word "media" is certainly a far-reaching and all-inclusive term these days. It wasn't always so. In my youth it mainly referred to the press, and all things printed — pamphlets, newspapers, magazines, and the like.

Then along came radio with the phenomenon of sound magically broadcast into homes via the airwaves. Radio stations were organized into networks, and those networks expanded into television when that technology arrived. Along the way, the sponsorship market grew and grew, advertising revenues justifying the expansion. Eventually, network TV pretty much left the airwaves to cable, and cable, with its seemingly limitless number of stations and programming, turned "the media" into an advertising bonanza surpassed only by the Internet.

I agree that this more recent form of electronic media is a marvel. It provides instant information about everything and everybody (with varying degrees of veracity). It also provides instant pop-up advertising everywhere, all the time. We're a long way from the era of commercial breaks and FCC-mandated public service announcements. The drive for advertising revenues has resulted in an era of less and less regulation.

I spent all my years in the business in broadcast media, not print media, and to me the difference is very significant. I can remember the days when our sports broadcasters association played second fiddle to newspapers. Press releases were written to coincide with when newspapers hit the streets, not when I was doing a broadcast. We all had to abide by the release time, whether it was 10 a.m. or 7 p.m. Often I wouldn't get a press release in time to use it on my show, and by my next opportunity, the story was already out in print. Newspapers had the advantage. Now, there are press releases all the time, but newspapers have decidedly lost their advantage. Additionally, press conferences are now much more popular, benefitting the electronic media, which can be there with bells and whistles. Great for us. Not so great for the print guys.

Those print guys were some of my closest pals. I had very good relations with my colleagues in the television business, but the print guys? Well, we hung out. Veteran Western New York broadcasters Ralph Hubbell and Chuck Healy both started out in print. They shared much of what they knew about the business, and I learned plenty from them. They were thorough in their approach; they paid attention to the details. They worked their sources. They honed their story until it was right. Sports writers Cy Kritzer, Joe Alli, and Phil Ranallo of the *Courier-Express*, hockey writer Dick Johnston, and a bunch of others were no different. They were all great people who loved what they were doing. I think that was probably what made them all so competent. Some of them were truly great writers. Ranallo had no peer.

Others became more than colleagues; they became close personal friends. Milt Northrop, Charlie Barton, and Mike Kanaley became cronies, pals, and even teachers. Steve Weller, a *Buffalo Evening News* columnist who ranked with the best in the country, was another, as were Larry Felser and Jim Peters. All these people in some way had a hand in writing this book; they were a big part of my education as a broadcaster. Good writers pour themselves into their work, and luckily, Buffalo continues to have great sports print journalists....maybe it's the Lake Erie water or the changing seasons that keep them at their best.

I regret what is happening to newspapers today. Many across the

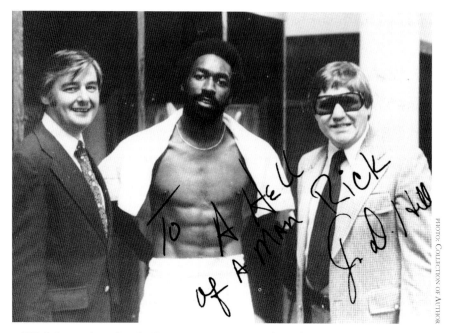

With legendary football writer Larry Felser (right) and Bills great, J. D. Hill. I let Larry ask all the questions.

country have already folded. Those hanging on have gone online in order to stay relevant. Now some of those "print" websites look a lot like TV. That might seem like a good idea, but in my opinion you can't take writers and make them into TV personalities.

Few regulations govern the broadcast media these days. That was not always the case. In my day, the FCC ruled the roost. Everyone in the business had to abide by its regulations — things like limits on how many stations one company could own and caps on how many commercials could be run in an hour. The Fairness Doctrine required stations to make every reasonable attempt to cover contrasting points of view. The FCC did away with that in 1987. Big mistake.

The flood gates have remained open. President Clinton signed the Telecommunications Act of 1996, which basically lifted the rules on corporate ownership. Formerly in radio, one company could own a maximum of forty stations. That's no longer the case. At last count, Clear Channel Communications owned twelve hundred stations. Other companies have expanded as well.

So what? You might say. Plenty, is the answer.

In today's hot political environment, those twelve hundred stations can and do promote the owners' own agendas. Balanced reporting is a thing of the past. News coverage has become generic, and the owners control what people throughout the country see and hear. There is only an appetite for controversy, which is often manufactured. As a result, a lot of stories are not being written. I fear the art of journalism, practiced by those I have admired, will soon be forgotten.

The losers are us.

People in My Profession

In my youth, I listened to the radio (believe it or not, there was no TV then), hoping that one of the local sports announcers —

Roger Baker, Jim Wells, Charley Bailey, Ralph Hubbell — would carry a score from my high school.

I never got to know Roger Baker, who for a time was the voice of the Cincinnati Reds; he returned to his home town of Buffalo in the '40s to continue his broadcasting career. Nor did I know Jim Wells, an announcer for WBEN, who had great delivery; I really enjoyed his style. He later moved to Arizona. But I did get to know Charley and Hub. Charley was with WEBR and eventually ended up in print at the *Courier-Express*. Stories about him are legendary.

Ralph worked at most of the radio and TV stations in town at one time or another. He had an approach unlike others of his era. While a lot of guys were blasting out the scores with punchy delivery, Ralph was always composed and thoughtful. He also wrote several books and occasionally contributed columns to the local print weeklies. He founded the Western New York Sports Broadcasters Association; its monthly meetings often featured guests of local and national repute. Members included the likes of Chuck Healy, Hubbell's colleague at WBEN, and Bill Mazer, a veteran broadcaster with WGR.

Ralph was a member of the inaugural class of the Greater Buffalo Sports Hall of Fame. We were already good friends by that time, and he had a hand in molding my attitude toward my job and its responsibilities. I suspect he had the same effect on Van Miller and Ed Kilgore, my longtime television compatriots at WBEN and WGRZ. Ralph was "the dean;" he set the tone. When he passed away in September 2000, Buffalo lost a broadcasting great and a class act.

We often talked about going elsewhere. Ralph never really wanted to go anywhere. He truly loved Buffalo. Van never left. I remember welcoming Ed at Mother's, a local emporium known for its libations, after work one day and telling him he would probably be around for a long time. He laughed, thinking otherwise. But he never left either. I came close a couple of times — once to Chicago, once back to NBC, and another time to ABC. I was already doing some weekend stuff for ABC Radio when a job opened up for weekdays. I only wanted to do the weekends, to fit in with my Channel 7 work during the week, but Howard Cosell, who was ABC's sports director at the time, wanted me to be there full time. I turned it down, just as I did the Chicago gig.

Cosell was like no one I had ever known. ABC Television's *Monday Night Football* — with Cosell, "Dandy" Don Meredith, and Frank Gifford, who replaced Keith Jackson, the original play-by-play guy — was a huge hit. This group was doing a Thursday night game in Buffalo a couple of years after I first met Cosell.

Edith and I with Howard Cosell. He was never at a loss for words.

The game started at 8 o'clock, not at 9 o'clock like Monday games. As I walked into the press box, there was Pat McGroder, a very special personal friend and a long-time Bills executive, talking with Cosell, who looked a little distressed. He immediately asked me what time the last plane for New York City left Buffalo International Airport. I replied, "Around 9 p.m."

Cosell then looked even more distraught. Apparently he had some important business in New York City that couldn't wait until morning. I suggested he get in touch with Prior Aviation, which offered charters. I said the owner, Jack Prior, was a friend.

"Would you call him for me?" Cosell asked. Armed with some

details, I made the call. Prior was at the game and not available, so I requested that the company have a plane ready to take off around midnight for Mr. Cosell of ABC. They called me back to say that a plane and pilot would be available. Explaining the details to Cosell, I mentioned that the plane would arrive in New York City around 3 a.m.

"What? Why so long? Isn't it a jet?" asked Cosell.

Back on the phone, I requested a jet. One was available, so Dandy Don and Frank also hitched a ride, and ABC picked up the tab.

A year later, I was in Texas to do a preseason game. Paul Maguire and I were taping some pregame stuff on the broadcast deck when Howard Cosell popped his head through a window. He stared at me, then smiled and after a few moments said: "Buffalo. Rick, I'll never forget what you did for me. Any time I can do something for you, let me know."

The guy remembered everything; he really did. I never took advantage of his offer, but I did spend time with him later and saw him at his best as well as his worst. He could put down anything or anybody in a split second. An example: When Bill Mazer got to New York in 1964 for a job at WNBC, he already had some good connections. But shortly after his arrival he met Cosell at Toots Shor's, the famous midtown hangout popular with celebrities from the '40s through the '60s. Cosell's welcoming statement was: "Don't unpack your bags, kid." But Mazer enjoyed a long and successful career in New York City, developing the sports talk radio format heard today.

Once, Cosell was the guest of honor at a luncheon sponsored by Channel 7. My boss told me I was to be the master of ceremonies. Dreading what Cosell might say, I tried to get out of it. Cosell's style was to criticize and disparage, and he enjoyed it. What to do? For all his celebrity and mountains of work, Cosell had never won an Emmy, TV's answer to the Oscar, but his wife was named Emmy. I made reference to his lack of Emmys during my introduction, but added: "He doesn't need one; he already has one, his wife, Emmy, and she's sitting right over there."

We became pals. Sometime later, I hosted the ABC special *A Day in the Life of Howard Cosell*.

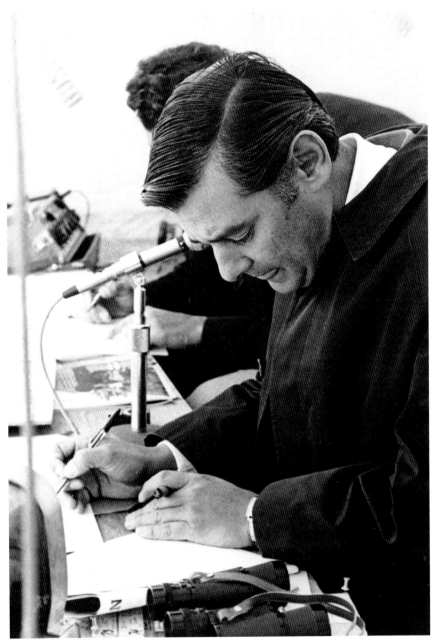

Covering an AFL-era Bills' game by paying attention to
the smallest details.

5
PIGSKIN TALES

PRO FOOTBALL IN BUFFALO

What we now call the NFL's first season officially occurred in 1920, although professional football's origins predate that. Fourteen teams were listed in the American Professional Football Association, which changed its name to the National Football League two years later. One of those original fourteen teams was named the Buffalo All-Americans. Only two of the group survived: the Decatur Staleys (now the Chicago Bears) and the Chicago Cardinals (now the Arizona Cardinals, after a stop in St. Louis). Buffalo stayed in the league for ten years, operating under the additional names of Bisons and Rangers. But after the 1929 season, that was it for quite some time.

The next serious shot at pro ball for Buffalo came in 1946 when the All-America Football Conference came to life. Jim Breuil, owner of Buffalo's Frontier Oil Company, footed the bill to get into the risky business of owning a football team in a newly formed league competing against the established NFL. The first head coach was Clem Crowe, who'd had a successful career coaching basketball and football in midwestern colleges, including Notre Dame. He soon gave way to Lowell Potter "Red" Dawson, who'd coached an undefeated season at Tulane and would go on to win Pittsburgh's "Dapper Dan" sports award. Dawson coached the All-America Football Conference Bills for most of their existence.

The original teams in the AAFC were the New York Yankees, the Brooklyn Dodgers, the Cleveland Browns, the San Francisco 49ers, the Los Angeles Dons, the Chicago Rockets, the Miami Seahawks, and the Buffalo Bisons. A year later, wanting to depart from "Bisons" as he sought a new identity for his AAFC team, Breuil held an essay contest to rename the Buffalo team. The winning essay made reference to the team as the "new frontier" in local sports and argued that the team should be named after the famous frontiersman Buffalo Bill Cody. Breuil must have liked this, perhaps because it played off the name of his company. The name "Bills" won. My brother and I never missed a game.

After a bitter feud with the NFL, and with almost all of their teams losing money, the AAFC disbanded in 1949, with the Browns, 49ers, and Baltimore Colts being picked up by the NFL. Even though the Bills were one of the better teams in the league, Buffalo was ignored. This remains a controversial story, and the whole truth may never be known. But a number of factors worked against Buffalo: the NFL rules required a unanimous vote, and

George Halas, owner of the Chicago Bears, was opposed. Also, Civic Stadium was not considered a good venue for an NFL team (the stadium issue again). But the rejection by the NFL was most painful to fans because the Colts were the worst team in the league, having won only one game in the 1949 season, the same year the Bills played the Browns for the AAFC championship. That version of the Colts lasted only one year in the NFL before disbanding (the current Colts franchise came about in 1953 as a result of the NFL's expansion).

What would have happened had the Bills made it to the NFL in 1950? The Browns' early success in the NFL is well documented. It's not difficult to surmise that the Bills would have been successful too. They had guys like George Ratterman, Chet Mutryn, Tom Colella (a Canisius College grad), Abe Gibron, Ed "Buckets" Hirsch, Vince Mazza from Niagara Falls, Rocco Pirro, and many others. Not only were they good football players, they also sounded like football players, with names like that. Many of the Bills from that team ended up in Cleveland, making the Browns even better than they already were.

It took ten years for Buffalo to get back into pro football. The American Football League was launched in 1960, and one of the original organizers was Michigan businessman Ralph Wilson. Wilson had his choice of where to form a team, including Buffalo,

Cincinnati, Miami, and at least two other locations. Wilson went to Miami, but that effort bore no fruit. He looked to Buffalo next and didn't have to search any further for a site to field his new AFL franchise. Wilson has kept the Bills in Buffalo for fifty-four years and counting. He is the league's longest-tenured owner. Wilson gets his share of criticism when the team doesn't win. That goes with the territory. But the fans in Buffalo should be forever grateful to him for his decision to play here and stay here. It's hard to imagine the City of Buffalo without its beloved Bills.

Before talking about the Buffalo Bills team, I would be remiss if I didn't advise fans to get a copy of Scott Pitoniak's *Buffalo Bills Football Vault*. It's a marvelous history of the team's first fifty seasons. That's number one. After that, add to your Bills library by picking up one or more of the many other books published about the team and its players — some written by the players and coaches themselves. I'd recommend Joe DeLamielleure's *Tales from the Buffalo Bills*, Sal Maiorana's *Complete Illustrated History* with a foreword by Steve Tasker, and *The Unofficial Buffalo Bills Book of Lists* by Larry Bump and Mike Doser. Hall of Fame coach Marv Levy, who was with the Bills from 1986 to 1997 and again from 2006 to 2007, has written about his Bills and has also authored a novel about the game.

ON COACHING

The Bills have had seventeen head coaches since their inception in 1960. Buster Ramsey was the first. At this writing, Doug Marrone is the latest. Several stand out. Most do not. A few had success. Most did not. It's been my privilege to know several Bills coaches. As the saying goes: I never met a coach I didn't like — personally. Professionally, however, is another matter.

I really didn't know Buster Ramsey; I hardly even interviewed him. Covering sports was only part of my duties at Channel 7 during his coaching tenure. In those days, before the Irv, Rick, and Tom era, and before my time as sports director, we did whatever was necessary to stay on the air.

Four Bills coaches make a short list of those with winning records: Lou Saban, Chuck Knox, Marv Levy, and Wade Phillips. Saban, Knox, and Levy all have received Coach of the Year honors from at least one major news organization. Knox's winning record was by one game, 37 wins to 36 losses. Saban was twice named Coach of the Year in the premerger AFL in 1964 and 1965, the years the Bills won the AFL championship. Knox received honors in 1980 (Associated Press, *Sporting News*, and *Pro Football Weekly*), and Marv Levy, of course, was inducted into the Pro Football Hall of Fame in Canton, Ohio, in 2001, among his many other honors. I met them all, but in Phillips's case, we were only casual acquaintances. He came along after I had retired. Nice man. Smart coach.

Saban, Knox, and Levy became pals, sort of. In my former profession, being pals with any head coach was anathema. Sports reporters couldn't allow personal feelings to interfere with their reporting, and it was believed that having friendly relationships with sources might compromise objectivity. In my case, it never did. I had some differences of opinion with a couple of them, but that never hurt our professional relationship. Establishing trust was always a challenge, especially with a guy like Jim Ringo. Not many in the press got close to him. I'll talk about him shortly.

Coaching is a unique profession. It takes someone who can effectively deal with a multitude of priorities, both on and off the field, but who is ultimately judged only by results in the win-loss column. Coaches need to instruct and motivate players and keep owners happy. And they need to satisfy the fans, whose confidence in a coach can change with the outcome of any one of hundreds of decisions that take place on game day. It ain't easy. For the most part, when it comes to the press, coaches are not trusting souls. How can they be? Their destiny is already defined. Sooner or later they're going to get fired.

LOU SABAN

Saban, who had coached the New England Patriots for a season and a half (he was fired five games into his second season), became the Bills' coach in 1962. Now this was a character. Very likeable, but you never knew what he might say or do next. I'll give you three examples, not in chronological order.

I was sitting in the announcers' booth at our Channel 7 studios, which were on Main Street at the time. In comes Saban, who plops down in a chair next to me and announces: "I think I'm going to quit."

I was stunned and thought I had a scoop in the making. I asked why he would quit. When he answered, he was dead serious: "Why? After the season we had, he won't even pay for my country-club dues."

"He" was Ralph Wilson, of course. I calmed Saban down and he waited a couple of years before quitting.

Another incident occurred in the early days, when the Bills were still at the Rockpile. The team had just lost to Houston by a couple of points. Everyone had left the Buffalo locker room — all the coaches, all the players, and all the reporters except me. I was in the dressing room on the second level, gathering together our equipment from the postgame interviews. I thought I was alone, but the door to the coaches' room suddenly swung open and Saban, bare naked, stormed out on his way to the shower. He stopped, saw me, and yelled, "Azar! Get in here!"

I followed the still-naked Saban back into the coaches' room, where I witnessed a tirade I thought would burst one of his blood vessels. I could guess why he was upset. They had lost. But now I was going to find out how and why he thought they had lost.

It was late in the fourth quarter of a closely contested game. The Bills were in possession, trailing the Houston Oilers 19 to 17, and they had driven the ball down to the Oilers' one-yard line. Buffalo's Pete Gogolak was sent out to kick the go-ahead points; a field goal at this point would have pretty much assured victory, assuming Buffalo could stop Houston from getting into scoring position on their ensuing possession. But the Bills suddenly turned around and quarterback Jack Kemp was sent back on the field to call a play, presumably to attempt a touchdown.

What was Saban thinking?

Sure enough, they did not score a touchdown; Kemp tried a quarterback sneak and was stopped short. The Bills lost the game. Everyone there must have thought Saban had blown it. But as I was about to find out, he was mad not only about the loss, but also how it came about.

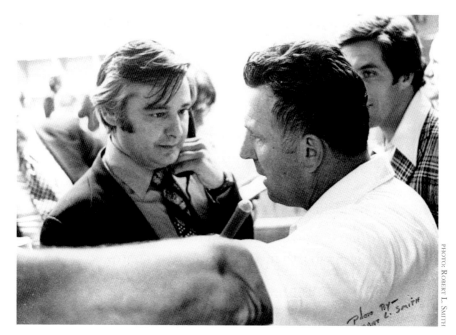

Interviewing Lou Saban in 1973. He was always candid.

Seems he had called for the field goal, but one of his assistants, running backs and receivers coach John Mazur, talked him out of it, reasoning that a Bills touchdown would force the Oilers to drive the length of the field, since they would then need a touchdown in order to win. They surely would not have enough time.

Saban fingered Mazur only to me. He never publicly berated Mazur in any way, but he excoriated him to me that afternoon, kicking lockers — with his bare feet — and using every profanity I had ever heard, and even some I hadn't.

"I'll never listen to an assistant coach again as long as I live!"

he shouted ("screamed" is probably a better description). I have often wondered why he trusted me not to use this story on the air. I considered it, to be sure, but decided it would not be in anyone's interest except my own. Certainly not Mazur's or Saban's, especially if I included the fact that all this occurred with Saban not wearing a stitch of clothing. Seems really funny now.

The third incident happened after another loss — and another missed scoring opportunity. We were doing Bills broadcasts on WKBW-AM radio at the time, during the 1970s. By "we" I mean myself, former WEBR broadcaster and Philadelphia Sports Hall of Fame inductee Al Meltzer, and former Bills receiver Eddie Rutkowski. Those years were incredibly fun, and a highlight for all of us.

I was doing a live interview of players after the 1976 home-opener loss against the Miami Dolphins, when Saban came into the room and sat down. I never even asked him a question. He just went on and on, lamenting the loss — due in part to three missed field goals — and giving everyone listening, including me, the idea that he was about to fire the kicker, John Leypoldt. Larry Felser, then covering the Bills for the *Buffalo Evening News*, later told me that people on their way home from the game had pulled their cars over to the side of the road to listen.

Thank goodness Saban didn't fire Leypoldt on the air, because

I had no idea what my follow-up question would have been. No doubt something dumb like, "Who's going to kick next week?" Seemed kind of cruel. Not to worry. It didn't happen, at least not on the air. He waited until the next day, and then he fired Leypoldt.

That was Saban: passionate, unpredictable, and a hell of a football coach.

Jim Ringo

By the time Jim Ringo arrived in Buffalo, he already had a huge reputation as one of the all-time-great offensive linemen to play in the NFL, earned as a member of the Green Bay Packers and the Philadelphia Eagles.

When he first came to the Bills in 1972 as the offensive line coach, he looked like he didn't have any friends and didn't want any. I tried to stay away from him. But as fate would have it, I arrived on a Saturday night for an away game in San Francisco sometime around 11 p.m. Though I normally traveled with the team, I had some previous commitments and had to fly in on my own. I headed straight to the hotel restaurant — not the fancy one but the coffee shop. There, sitting at the counter by himself, was Jim Ringo.

I nodded and softly said hello. He barely nodded back. I guessed he had pulled monitor duty — making sure all the players were safely tucked in by 11 p.m. — and suggested as much. He actually gave me an audible response in the affirmative. Now that we'd broken the ice, we continued to sip coffee and chat. Even though we were about five stools apart, we never moved closer. I wouldn't dare make such a move, and I already knew he wouldn't.

Little did I know that this small interaction was the beginning of a long-term friendship. It was clear to me that he didn't trust the media, and I'll admit I never knew exactly why, nor did I ask. But, at least in my case, he turned out to be a loyal friend. I came to understand why his players respected him. He was loyal to them, too. During Ringo's second stint with the Bills, in a 1987 game against Indianapolis, he was standing on the sidelines when a kickoff return came right at him. He couldn't get out of the way fast enough and ended up at the bottom of the pile — with a broken leg. He was carted off, put in a cast and, before you knew it, was back on the sidelines on crutches, urging his troops on. No wonder they loved the guy.

As a Bills assistant coach, Ringo masterminded the famous Electric Company offensive line, so named because it paved the way for running back O. J. Simpson and his rushing records — it was said to have "turned the Juice loose." He ended up as the head coach of the Bills, taking over for Saban in 1976, after Saban's second stint in that job. But Ringo was never cut out to be a head coach. During his tenure he coached twenty-three games and won only three. He was fired after his second season. I was the only reporter he talked to after that happened. Don't ask me why; I guess it was that loyalty thing again.

Ringo returned to the Bills as offensive coordinator from 1985 until his retirement from pro football in 1988, helping the team to the AFC championship game in his final year. He established the foundation of the Bills teams that went on to four consecutive Super Bowl appearances. Jim was inducted into the Pro Football Hall of Fame in 1981, and his name is rightfully on the Wall of Fame at Ralph Wilson Stadium. He passed away in 2007, and I will never forget his friendship and the lasting impact he had as both a player and a coach.

CHUCK KNOX

Chuck Knox was the next coach to come to Buffalo. He replaced Ringo and heads are still being scratched trying to figure out how Ralph Wilson got him in the first place. He had had a stellar run with the Los Angeles Rams. His teams had won five straight division championships, with ten or more victories each year.

With the Bills winning only a total of five games in the prior two seasons, Knox spent his first two years in Buffalo rebuilding. And what a job he and his staff — which included Norm Pollom, who eventually became the Bills' director of player personnel — did drafting new talent. Among the players who came to Buffalo were Terry Miller, Lucius Sanford, Jerry Butler, Fred Smerlas, Jim Haslett, Jeff Nixon, Rod Kush, Jim Ritcher, Joe Cribbs, and Mark Brammer. The team became very competitive and began having winning seasons after Knox's first two years.

All-American linebacker Tom Cousineau from Ohio State was the top pick in 1979, but he never put on a Bills uniform, opting instead to join the Montreal Alouettes. There are all kinds of stories as to why he never came to Buffalo. Montreal had offered double the money; that might have had something to do with it. General manager Stew Barber and Knox did not always see eye-to-eye, and while I do not know their respective opinions on Cousineau, I believe Knox was disappointed with that whole situation. What I know for a fact is that he planned to fulfill his contract in Buffalo and then go elsewhere after the 1982 season. I used that story in 1979. Nobody believed me. But Knox told me this himself.

After Knox declared publically that he was leaving, he didn't say where he was going, and no NFL team made any announcements. That left the whole town wondering where he was off to. It was clear he would be coaching somewhere. One station had him going back to the Rams. I predicted he'd head for Seattle, which is where he ended up as their new head coach for the 1983 season. How did I know?

I had called Kay Stephenson, the Bills' newly appointed head coach, at home. After all, he'd been on Knox's staff in both L.A. and Buffalo. I asked if he knew where Knox was headed. He said, "Just a minute." The next voice I heard was Knox's. He happened to be visiting Stephenson, trying to get him to go with him to his new job. "Where would that be?" I asked. "Seattle," he responded.

There's nothing like being able to trust your sources.

Most of the players loved Knox. He was their kind of guy, a tough, no-nonsense type. But the quarterbacks seemed to be slightly less fond of him than the others. I really think Knox would just as soon play the game without a quarterback. He didn't have a whole lot of confidence in them — nor in receivers for that matter.

I used to have a running argument with Knox about Bobby Chandler, who I thought was a great receiver for the Bills, and Knox wasn't so convinced. I was at Knox's office taping a pregame segment when off camera Knox showed me a computer printout he had obtained in advance of their upcoming game against the Kansas City Chiefs. He proceeded to tell me: "This is the Kansas City scouting report on the Bills. I won't tell you how I got it, and if you tell anybody I have it, I'll deny the whole thing. You know what it says about the great Bobby Chandler? They rate him our fourth-best receiver. So there's your great Bobby Chandler."

Nevertheless, Knox used his knowledge of the Chiefs' lack of respect for Chandler and adapted the Bills' game plan accordingly. Chandler had over 100 yards receiving and two touchdown receptions in that game.

But Knox loved the down-and-dirty guys. I once asked Fred Smerlas, who had played for a number of different coaches, who his favorite was. He never skipped a beat. Chuck Knox, he told me.

When asked why, he told this story: "We were going to play the Vikings. Chuck comes up to me before the game and says, 'Fred, you're going up against one of the all-time-great centers today, Mick Tingelhoff. I want you to put your arm up his butt and pull his heart out.'" Smerlas paused, then continued: "I could identify with that."

For a player like Smerlas, that's the legacy of Chuck Knox.

STEPHENSON AND BULLOUGH

Instead of moving out West with Knox, Stephenson stayed on as head coach of the Bills, and for one season at least, it looked like he might have an extended stay. He finished 1983, his first season, at 8 to 8. The rest of his stay, however, was a disaster. His team won only two games in 1984 and started 1985 losing four in a row. I believed Stephenson had the talent to be the Bills' head coach. As a friend from his playing days with the AFL Bills, it was difficult for me to see him struggle. But after the slow start in Stephenson's third season, Ralph Wilson had had enough. Hank Bullough, the defensive coordinator, took over, and his team won two games during the rest of the season. His next season didn't go so well either. Bullough should never have become head coach. I don't think he had a good rapport with his team. No player spoke out in his defense when he was fired after a week-nine loss to Tampa Bay.

Edith and I had organized a group to travel to Tampa for that game; it was intended as a mix of a little work for me, and then a short vacation with some of our close friends. After doing several postgame interviews, I sensed that Bill Polian, who was now the general manager, had had enough of Bullough, but I never asked outright if he planned a coaching change. Instead, I inquired whether he thought I should return to Buffalo with the team instead of staying in Florida for a few days. All he said was, "I think that's a good idea."

Bullough was let go the next day. The Marv Levy era was about to begin.

MARV LEVY

I first met Marv Levy when Channel 7 hired him to be the color commentator for the Bills preseason telecasts. That was in the early 1980s, but by that time Marv had already had an illustrious career coaching collegiate football, the NFL, and the CFL, where his teams had won two championships. Marv was great as a television analyst, and I learned a lot from him. By mid-1986, he was the head coach of the Bills. Polian and Levy had worked together in Montreal (CFL Alouettes), Kansas City (NFL Chiefs), and Chicago (USFL Blitz), so they knew each other well. We had become good friends while we were working together and after he became head coach, we remained good friends, but now the relationship took on another dimension. We discussed the issue and he said: "I know you have a job to do; I understand that and it will never diminish our friendship."

When Levy took over the coaching reins, the team was already assembling a bunch of talented players, thanks to Polian's outstanding ability to assess football talent. Talented players usually have big egos, and the talent Polian had assembled was massive: Jim Kelly, Thurman Thomas, Andre Reed, Bruce Smith, et cetera, et cetera. Larry Felser, the *Buffalo News* columnist and a close friend, once commented that he could think of no other coach who could have handled that team. He was so right.

The Bills were becoming more successful under Levy. They posted a 12–4 season in 1988 and went to the AFC Championship game. The following season was a letdown; they still finished with a winning record at 9–7, but expectations, both inside and outside of the team, were much higher. Internal conflicts became public. Writers around the league were commenting about the so-called "bickering" Bills. The stories were endless about what Kelly said, or Thomas said, or what this guy or that guy was grumbling about. But that group of players, with the possible exception of Ron Harmon (he dropped an easy pass in the end zone against Cleveland that knocked the Bills out of the playoffs in 1989), are the best of friends even to this day. If you don't believe me, just ask them.

They won a record four straight AFC Championships and went to four straight Super Bowls. They didn't win any but, hey, a record is a record.

In May 1990, I got a call from Marv who asked if I would speak to the team about media relations at the start of training camp. At first I shuddered at the thought. Me, telling those guys how to handle the media?

I suggested to Marv that we hold the session during minicamp, before training camp. My thinking? Not as many people around — no media types, no guest coaches, no hangers-on. Perhaps the players would be relaxed and more open to suggestion. He said no. But five minutes later he called back and said, "Maybe you're right. Let's do it now."

Bills receiver and special teams ace Steve Tasker had been one of my interns at Channel 7. He had expressed interest in a TV career after football, and I was happy to bring him on to help him learn the ropes. I bounced the idea off him. He thought it was a great idea and would ask the first question to get things going.

I made a little speech about the team and bickering problems and how that stuff should be kept in-house. "The Steelers call themselves a family," I said. "That's how you should feel about yourselves. You and your brothers and sisters fought amongst yourselves too, but let an outsider lay a hand on any of them or say anything derogatory about them and you were there to defend them. That's what this team should be about. Trust each other and know who you can trust on the outside."

Steve asked the first question, and an hour later we were through. To be sure, they still had their moments afterwards, but I'd like to think that morning was the beginning of the end of bickering.

BILL POLIAN

Bill Polian wasn't a Bills coach, but he certainly deserved the honor of recently being placed on the Buffalo Bills Wall of Fame.

Speaking with Chuck Knox at Bills' training camp in the early 1980s.
Here he displays his usual pensive look.

Bill Polian, Bills' GM, and me celebrating a big win after the Bills beat
the Raiders in the 1991 AFC Championship game on the way to their
first Super Bowl appearance. He told his wife: "I've got the best team
in the league."

He has already been elected to the Greater Buffalo Sports Hall of Fame as the architect of the most famous football team in Bills history. He and Levy formed the finest GM/coach partnership I ever witnessed.

How does one express what Bill Polian meant to the Buffalo Bills or any other organization he has been associated with, including the Carolina Panthers and the Indianapolis Colts? He took a ragtag Colts team and built it into a Super Bowl champion. He built the Panthers into a Super Bowl contender in the second year of their existence, the fastest I can recall of any expansion team. They went all the way to the NFC championship game.

He rose from his first job with the Bills as director of pro personnel to general manager, and signed Jim Kelly (after he'd spurned the Bills in 1983 to play in the fledgling USFL). He's the guy who had the foresight to hire the intellectual, writer, and historian Marv Levy as head coach. The team Polian built with Levy became one of the most successful of the 1990s.

Like Saban, Polian was a volatile leader while he was in Buffalo. He had his scrapes with the media, the league, and anyone who disagreed with him. During a speech in front of the Bills Monday Quarterback Club, he famously admonished some writers to "get out of town" if they didn't like his modus operandi. I called him the next day, applying (tongue in cheek) for what I thought would be the vacant position of speech writer. He laughed, and we have been friendly ever since.

But being a GM is often like coaching: eventually, you get fired. After a devastating defeat at the hands of the Dallas Cowboys in Super Bowl XXVII, Polian got into a shouting match with a local TV sports director, and I had to separate the two before they came to fisticuffs. Soon after that he was fired and went on to bigger and better things in North Carolina and Indianapolis. But Bills fans have never forgotten him and what he did for the team, and neither has Ralph Wilson, apparently, since he approved Polian's ascension to the Wall of Fame.

The Players

Paul Maguire

One hour before broadcast is a busy time in any TV newsroom in the country. So it was at Channel 7. One July evening so many years ago that the Bills training camp was still housed at Niagara University, the phone rang. It was Bills punter Paul Maguire calling. He told me he was lonely. And he proceeded to try to convince me to say good night on-air to all the poor players who felt abandoned because they didn't have enough sheets to tie together so they could sneak out of the sixth floor players' dormitory after curfew.

Funny? Yeah. But I was in the hectic phase, readying my broadcast. Still, the more I thought about it, the bigger my smile. This was something I could use. That night, on my sports broadcast, out came the story about the sad life of timid football players, who were so captive and lonely without their mommies around to tuck them in at night. Maguire became a hero; I became a pal.

After his retirement, I thought he would make a good color man on our preseason telecasts. I was right. Here's a quick highlight: Maguire was doing the color on a Steelers game when Bubby Brister was their quarterback. Steelers are on their own 45 in a shotgun formation. The center bounces the snap. Brister picks it up and laterals to a running back, who drops the ball, picks it up, and laterals it back over to Brister, who then throws a pass to a receiver, who catches it on the 10-yard line.

Without missing a beat, Maguire says: "I saw that play in the parking lot just before the game. It was the exact same play, except the guy in the parking lot was holding a hot dog when he made the catch."

Maguire had a long career as a color commentator for the networks. He makes me laugh like no one else and is one of my dearest friends.

JACK KEMP

Shortly after it was announced in 1962 that the Bills had acquired a fellow named Jack Kemp, a quarterback with a broken finger, I got a call from Dr. Morley Bernstein, an orthopedic physician who practiced in Niagara Falls. Being from the Falls, my wife knew him, and he was already a friend. He invited me to lunch.

I accepted the invitation, and, lo and behold, when I arrived, I found that a third party had been invited — Jack Kemp.

Doc may or may not have been a sports nut. Perhaps he decided not to take any chances, so he brought one on board (me) to make conversation. This was a social meeting, not a business meeting. No interviews. But still, I needed to do my job.

The San Diego Chargers had placed Kemp on waivers, thinking no team would claim him with that broken finger. Wrong.

The Bills list of starting QBs preceding Kemp is, well, less than legendary: Bob Brodhead, Al Dorow, Johnny Green, Richie Lucas, Warren Rabb, M. C. Reynolds. The team was desperate and took a chance that Kemp's finger would heal quickly. Jack was a pleasant guy, trying to get his busted digit better, so that made him anxious. Understandable.

I would later find out that he was intense and competitive throughout his athletic career. I guess you have to be to play football, especially if you're a quarterback. Kemp was not the most talented quarterback to play for the Bills. He had a strong arm, but he could be inconsistent, hot one game, cold the next. It was not an easy ride. The Bills drafted a gunslinger named Daryle Lamonica in 1963. Kemp and Lamonica would compete for the quarterback position, and that bothered Kemp immensely.

Fans these days love a quarterback controversy, but this one was a doozy. The Rob Johnson versus Doug Flutie debate during the late 1990s pales in comparison. The fans' fickle finger came to light; many favored the back-up Lamonica over the veteran Kemp. And Lamonica had his successes, coming in for Kemp to secure a few victories. But Kemp got his due. In a game that Lamonica had started, he was replaced by Kemp in the middle of a drive. The boos in the Rockpile were deafening and continued even as Kemp faded back to throw a TD pass. In an instant, the boos changed to cheers. In 1964 and 1965, Kemp led the team to two straight AFL championships against the Chargers, the team that had let him go.

Kemp retired from football in 1969 and, to the surprise of no one who knew him, turned to politics. Kemp had been active in Republican circles during his playing days. He had a way with all types of people, and his teammates from that era would attest to his leadership skills. He was elected to Congress (my wife worked on his first campaign), ran for vice president on a ticket with Bob

Dole in 1996, and remained a political force until his death in 2009. Our political views couldn't have been more different, but he was a long-time friend.

COOKIE GILCHRIST

Okay, I'll say it. Cookie Gilchrist was the best all-around football player I ever saw play, and I know several respected football journalists who agree with me, including Larry Felser and Jim Peters.

Ex-college and pro football coach Tom Harp thinks so, too. He told me about the time, prior to his professional playing days, when Cookie tried to enroll in Washington High School in Massillon, Ohio. Nobody calls it Washington High; everybody calls it Massillon. They have a 20,000-seat stadium in a town of 30,000 people. Legends have coached there (Paul Brown, for example). The team's winning percentage is also legendary. It seemed as though Cookie had made a good choice, but Massillon didn't want him. I guess they were too powerful already. After Paul Brown attempted to get him to play for the Cleveland Browns, Cookie ended up in the Canadian Football League, playing for several teams there as an All-Star runner and linebacker.

In 1962, the Bills director of player personnel, Harvey Johnson, signed Cookie to an AFL contract with Buffalo. He took the league by storm, becoming its first 1,000-yard rusher in 1962 and setting a single-game rushing record of 243 yards. He was an awesome runner.

Cookie always thought he was underpaid. He was constantly devising schemes (legal) to make more money. It finally got him on the wrong side of owner Ralph Wilson. That may be what has kept him from a place on the Wall of Fame.

Cookie also had some run-ins with the law. He was not a drinker and was not known to be a carouser. He lived on Humboldt Parkway, which was one of Buffalo's most beautiful streets until the Kensington Expressway came along in the mid-1960s. He went through a stop sign near his home, and the police were there to ticket him. One thing led to another. Words were exchanged. Cookie thought he was being harassed and argued until he got arrested. Off they all went to the police station. One officer apparently grabbed Cookie's arm to move him somewhere, and Cookie gave him a shove. The officer landed on the floor against a wall, and Cookie landed in jail.

When his case came up before the grand jury, guess who was sitting on the jury? Me.

The prosecution wanted me off the case, and I offered to step down. The sheriff objected. So I heard all of the proceedings, but

Jack Kemp, the quarterback who could have been president.

At a Monday Quarterback Club luncheon with Paul Maguire and Bill Polian. Paul has always found a way to make me laugh.

did not vote. His lawyers got him off anyway, something about double jeopardy.

I talked with Cookie several times, as recently as a month or so before his death in 2011. He wanted so much to be on the Wall of Fame and had written to Mr. Wilson. I don't know if he will ever get there, but he is a member of the Greater Buffalo Sports Hall of Fame and will forever be remembered for his uncompromising style, both on and off the field.

O. J. Simpson

Buffalo Bills radio broadcasts had long been the property of WBEN. Then, one day, Norm Schrutt, the boss across the parking lot at WKBW radio, announced that KB had won the rights to broadcast the Bills games.

Schrutt put together the team of Al Meltzer, Eddie Rutkowski, and me. What a ride we had. This was in the '70s, at the height of O. J. Simpson's career.

It was a perfect match.

Jeff Kaye was our producer, and boy was he good. He not only produced the games, he also had me in the studio on Mondays to narrate a program of the weekend games complete with music, highlights, and interviews. We did this through the 1977 season,

Broadcasting the Bills games on WKBW radio in the mid-'70s with my pal and former Bills receiver Eddie Rutkowski.

after which KB gave up the rights, and WBEN picked them up again. Van Miller, who previously had the play-by-play duties, got his old job back.

Al, Eddie, and I saw every inch of every yard O. J. ran to break NFL great Jim Brown's long-standing single-season rushing record. He did it on December 16, 1973, against the Jets at Shea stadium, breaking the 2,000-yard barrier. Offensive guard Reggie McKenzie was the catalyst. After O. J. passed Brown's mark of 1,863 yards, Reggie said in the huddle, "Let's go for 2,000." They did.

At Shea Stadium on December 16, 1973, when O. J. Simpson set an NFL single season rushing record of 2,003 yards. I got the first interview.

Edith and Eddie's wife, Mary Lou, traveled with us to the game and watched this momentous event from the press box restaurant. In spite of being populated with Jets fans, everyone there stood and cheered as the new record was achieved.

I was fortunate to have the first interview with O. J. after that game, and our broadcast of that historic NFL moment is part of a permanent display at the Pro Football Hall of Fame in Canton, Ohio. O. J.'s single season rushing record has since been surpassed; subsequent running backs have had the advantage of a regular season schedule that was lengthened from fourteen to sixteen games in 1978. However, as of this writing, no other NFL player has rushed for more than 2,000 yards in just fourteen games.

It's regrettable that O. J. has had some monumental problems since then. The glitter of his accomplishments for the Bills and his extraordinary talent as a running back have essentially been washed away as a result. But the fact remains that O. J. Simpson was one of the best who ever played the game.

Joe Namath

When you predict your team's victory in the Super Bowl, you become a big-time celebrity. The victory I'm referring to, of course, was when the Jets, led by Namath as quarterback, beat the Colts in the 1969 Super Bowl. Many laughed at the audacity of this Pennsylvania native who went to school in Alabama, when he responded to a heckler by saying he "guaranteed" his team would win — until the final score: Jets 16, Colts 7.

Joe Namath was already a household name when Edith and I got to know him. We were in Fort Lauderdale, Florida, on a short, spring golf vacation when we ran into Marty Schottenheimer, who played linebacker for the Bills. He was exiting the pro shop at the Diplomat Country Club as I was going in to reserve a tee time for the next day.

We went through the usual banter, and he asked me if I knew Joe Namath, who was sitting in the car waiting for Schotzy.

That meeting turned into several golf dates, and a friendship developed. I would see Namath on my trips to New York City, have dinner from time to time, and even paid a visit to his Manhattan apartment.

A couple of years later we were in Fort Lauderdale again. Namath spent time there during the off-season, so naturally we scheduled a $10 Nassau golf game. While we were waiting to tee off, a gentleman who I assumed was coming over to greet Namath approached us. Instead he stopped in front of me and asked if I was Rick Azar. The guy had no idea that Joe Namath was standing right next to me.

One of the highlights of my career.

THE STADIUM

When I was a kid growing up on Ellicott Street on the near east side of Buffalo, the area was very proud of its open-air sports venue. Many events were hosted at Civic Stadium, from midget auto racing and outdoor professional boxing to college and professional football. I remember when Canisius College upset heavily favored St. Bonaventure, which was then coached by the legendary Hugh Devore, and when Duke played one of its regular season football games there. The AAFC Bills played in the stadium and the AFL Bills began life there. But even after the addition of around ten thousand seats in 1960, the venue fell short of the 50,000-seat capacity required after the merger of the AFL and NFL.

Time to build a new stadium. The Erie County legislature dragged its feet, but finally agreed on a $50 million bond issue to get the work started. I had supported the idea in an editorial, and so did the *Buffalo Evening News*. Paul Neville, the *News*' editor at the time, called to thank me for my position. I had never spoken to him about the issue.

Enter the Kenford Company, owned by local developer Edward H. Cottrell. Kenford had acquired options on property in suburban Lancaster with the intention of making a deal with the county to build and manage a geodesic-domed stadium. The *Buffalo Courier-Express* opposed Kenford's plan, supporting a city location known as the Crossroads site. Then a third plan was proposed. The Greater Buffalo Chamber of Commerce formed a committee, and architectural firms from Buffalo and Atlanta jointly submitted plans for a football-only venue, a multipurpose edifice (football and baseball), and two stadiums side by side, as in Kansas City. The site for this third scenario would most likely have been in suburban Amherst. Arguments about the three locations: Lancaster, Buffalo, and Amherst abounded. Friends stopped talking to one another.

Where did it get built? In Orchard Park. Go figure.

Kenford entered into an agreement with the county to donate the land in Lancaster in exchange for an affiliated company, Dome Stadium, Inc., obtaining a forty-year lease to the new facility. All along, Ralph Wilson voiced opposition to dealing with anyone outside the Erie County legislature. He was also pushing for a stadium with significantly greater capacity than that planned by Kenford. The county panicked and fumbled. Instead of working a deal agreeable to all parties, legislators ran in the opposite direction and abandoned the domed stadium idea and the Lancaster location altogether. Kenford eventually sued for breach of contract and won a record settlement.

The proposed domed stadium would probably have seated, at most, around 65,000 people. Wilson wanted 80,000-seat capacity. The "smart" guys (including me) snickered. No one thought the area could support a stadium of that size. But while the geodesic dome would have given the area a unique identity, Wilson knew that capacity — and resulting ticket revenues — can mean the difference between success and failure for a NFL franchise. Thus was born what is now known as Ralph Wilson Stadium, or simply The Ralph, in suburban Orchard Park. Some people complain about its location — that it's too far out of town, and there are always traffic jams on game day. Fair enough. But it still offers the most affordable ticket in the league and has the best sightlines. While hindsight makes people smart, foresight is better, and Ralph Wilson had it.

HOW THE GAME HAS CHANGED

I don't know about you, but I'm a draftnik. That's somebody who does his homework thinking he can outguess all those smart GMs and coaches, because he knows what his team needs and doesn't need. But my oh my, how the draft has changed. Now it's a big deal, nationally televised on ESPN and lasting three days — an honest-to-goodness extravaganza that even causes family arguments.

I was at the Bills' offices in the Statler Hotel when they made their first pick in the 1969 draft.

Harvey Johnson was the man in charge. I showed up, the only reporter to witness — live — this momentous occasion.

Harvey directed me to a small office and sat down at a desk with one phone on it. We chatted, both knowing whom the Bills would choose, but he did not talk about that.

After about fifteen minutes of small talk, the phone rang. Harvey answered, identifying himself. The tension was almost unbearable. Finally, he said, "The Buffalo Bills select O. J. Simpson."

That was it. He hung up. He didn't even say goodbye.

Compare that with what goes on today. The information highway is flooded with data on hundreds of potential players. We draftniks become privy to how often a guy shaves in a week, never mind how fast he can run. The stuff is all over the Internet.

I often think about that 1969 draft, not because of O. J., but because of the extraordinary path the NFL has traveled in becoming a huge industry. I remember the days when Jack Kemp and his fellow players had to get off-season jobs to make ends meet. It took some time before Kemp would make $50,000 in one season and not need to moonlight. Now, draft day produces instant millionaires.

Professional team sports are multibillion dollar businesses these days. Players make enough money in one season to last a lifetime. No off-season jobs for them. During the AFL days, many of the Bills players were my personal friends. I never let it interfere with my job. We were all working men, with little difference in income, so we had much in common socially. The salaries professional athletes command now and the attention paid to them make such relationships difficult, perhaps impossible.

Nobody in football plays both offense and defense anymore. They used to. Pro pitchers seldom pitch a complete game unless they have a no-hitter in the works. Basketball has really grown up. I can remember when we had a six-foot-three-inch guy playing center. Now he plays guard — maybe.

The positive aspect of all this is that professional athletes are bigger, better, and more gifted than ever before. And they are getting paid for it — deservedly so. College athletics are another story.

BOWL FRENZY

Whatever happened to college sports? A quick answer: They became big business, particularly football and basketball. But I'll focus on football.

In 1906, the Intercollegiate Athletic Association of the United States was formed. It resulted from a conference of college officials called by then President Theodore Roosevelt to reconsider dangerous and exploitative practices in college athletics. The need for change was especially true for football, a rugged and unsupervised game that caused many injuries and even deaths.

By 1910, the IAA became known as the National Collegiate Athletic Association. The association wasn't a big business then, but more like a supervisory club dealing with rules and regulations. It still is. But more committees were formed, leading to tournaments in basketball and a national championship by 1939. The fan base exploded. Even with the emergence of the NFL, the popularity of college football continued to grow. The National Junior College Athletic Association was formed in 1938 and the National Association of Intercollegiate Athletics, in 1940, and many major and smaller conferences followed.

I remember when most football fanatics were glued to the radio, and later television, on New Year's Day to take in the Rose Bowl, which started in 1902 as the East-West game played in Pasadena. When other bowl games came along in the 1930s, including the Sugar, Orange, and Cotton bowls, the best college football teams were invited. One recent January, I counted thirty-five licensed bowl games. In addition to traditional games, bowls were named for Chick-Fil-A, Outback, Buffalo Wild Wings, Little Caesers Pizza, Famous Idaho Potato, and dozens of others. The names change at a moment's notice. To fill out the bowl schedule, less-than-elite teams are invited to play, with sponsors paying millions of dollars to participating colleges. Advertising revenues feed the machine; it's big, big business. And I'm not even talking about the Bowl Championship Series, which until 2013 selected the top five end-of-season college football matchups. The series did nothing to determine a national champion. It was just another way to drive more money into those games. Thankfully, it's being replaced by a playoff. That, at least, is a good thing.

Crowding in for an April 1960 game during the final season of Bisons
baseball at Offermann Stadium.

6
BASEBALL DREAMS

BISONS NATION

Professional baseball has had a home in Buffalo since 1879, when the Bisons played in the National League. I learned that in Joe Overfield's gift to local fans, *The 100 Seasons of Buffalo Baseball*, a must-read for anyone interested in baseball and the rich history of my home town. That history includes a variety of teams and leagues until 1921, when Frank Offermann, once Erie County sheriff, and the Jacobs family, who own the hospitality management firm Delaware North Companies, took ownership of the International League Bisons. The Bisons played their home games in a wood-frame ballpark at East Ferry Street and Michigan Avenue until 1924, when it was replaced by a more modern stadium, originally called Bison Stadium, then renamed for Offermann after his death a decade later. Offermann Stadium served as the franchise's home until the Bisons moved into the Rockpile in 1960.

Offermann Stadium was the first baseball park outside of Brooklyn that I had ever been in. Frankly, I remember more about it than the famous one in Brooklyn. There's no Ebbets Field in Brooklyn anymore, and the one at Michigan and Ferry is gone, too.

In the '30s and '40s, every kid knew something about baseball, and even if you were the last guy chosen, you played. Everybody played. We all knew many of the major leaguers, but we knew everybody on the Bisons team.

The Bisons were the top minor league affiliate of the Detroit Tigers, and in those days there was no revolving door back and forth. Mayo Smith played center field for the Bisons forever, it seemed. He never got to the majors as a player, but he did become the Tiger's manager.

Luke Easter joined the Bisons when he was forty years old after a career in the majors with Cleveland. His feats in Buffalo are well documented by Overfield, who tells of the time Luke belted a ball over Offermann Stadium's center-field scoreboard, 60 feet high and 400 feet away.

I happened to be in the press box that night with Cy Kritzer of the *News* and Joe Alli of the *Courier-Express*. We were the only reporters at the game. Cy was the official league scorekeeper, and I'll never forget his reaction to the amazing play. The ball Luke hit seemed to float in the air with a tremendous afterburner. As it rose, Cy rose with it, slowly moving up and out of his seat with this look of amazement on his face. We were all stunned. It had never happened before. No one had come close.

That same night, June 14, 1957, Joe Caffie hit a sign next to the scoreboard but not over it. Two months later, Luke did it again.

Luke Easter was one of a kind.

Other names I remember from those early days as a young fan, and later as a reporter, include Ollie Carnegie, Lou Boudreau, Fred Hutchinson, Virgil (Fire) Trucks, Rufe Gentry, Bucky Harris, Mickey Rocco, Jimmy Outlaw, Eddy "Shovels" Kobesky, Saul Rogovin (who once pitched both ends of a doubleheader and won both games), and on and on, to a 19-year old catcher named Johnny Bench. Buffalo was the breeding ground for countless stars.

Plenty of superstars passed through here, too, though they didn't play for the Bisons. Jackie Robinson came to Buffalo as a member of the Montreal Royals. I had the pleasure of introducing him at a local banquet, a moment I will never forget.

I also remember the June 1948 day when the Bisons massacred Syracuse in both ends of a double header: 22–11, with ten home runs, and 16–12.

Many of us remember the filming of that great baseball movie, *The Natural*, at War Memorial Stadium in 1983. That's the same

Luke Easter swings for the center field scoreboard at Offermann Stadium, July 1959.

year Bob and Mindy Rich, of Rich Products Corporation, bought the team; what a ride it's been since then. The downtown ballpark the couple helped build was finished in time for the 1988 season. That year and the one that followed, the Bisons played before two million fans, more than several major league teams were able to draw.

I had some great times watching baseball in Buffalo. Today, Offermann Stadium is the site of the Buffalo Academy for the Visual and Performing Arts. Rather fitting, I think. It's also fitting that minor league baseball is alive and well in Buffalo thanks to the Riches and a former mayor, Jimmy Griffin, who supported construction of a new home for the Bisons.

Buffalonians are fortunate to have people like Bob and Mindy, who care so much about the community. They've kept their family business — one that is known worldwide — in the city. What an enormous plus they are for my hometown.

Luke vs. Satchel

There aren't too many fans left who remember the time Luke Easter faced off against Satchel Paige in Buffalo. Paige was a pitcher who worked mostly on Negro League teams, but eventually found his way into the majors with the Cleveland Indians. So did Luke Easter, who was a powerful hitter. After their days in the majors, they both returned to the minors. They knew the game's entertainment value.

A day came when Paige was pitching against Luke at Offermann Stadium. Paige had more varied pitches than most. He had a famous fastball and eventually figured out how to throw a curve. He also had a knuckler, a screwball, a hesitation pitch, and something he called an Eephus, which is a very low-speed "junk" pitch. Just watching Paige on the mound was a show in itself, and Luke, at six-four and well over 200 pounds, was quite a physical presence. I know Luke got at least one hit, because I remember the crowd going bananas.

Paige was the first player to be inducted into the Hall of Fame based on his play in the Negro Leagues, thanks in part to Ted Williams's 1966 Hall of Fame speech urging inclusion of Negro League players. Williams was that kind of guy.

I wonder how many of today's players have as much fun playing as Easter and Paige did.

JOE MCCARTHY

It takes an old-time baseball fan to remember a guy named Joe McCarthy. He was born in Philadelphia, attended Niagara University, and lived most of his life with his wife, Babe, on a farm bordering Ellicott Creek in Tonawanda. He played in the minor leagues, including a stop in Buffalo, but a severe knee injury kept him out of the majors. He turned his innate baseball talent to managing and was one of the great managers of all time, which eventually earned him a spot in the Baseball Hall of Fame in Cooperstown.

After leading Louisville to American Association championships in 1921 and 1925, he was hired by the Chicago Cubs. He got the Cubs to the World Series by 1929 but was let go the following year. The Yankees and the Boston Red Sox offered him contracts. He accepted the Yankees' offer and led them to seven World Series titles during his sixteen seasons in pinstripes. After leaving New York, he guided the Red Sox to second-place finishes in 1948 and '49, missing out on the pennant by a single game each season.

Several times, around World Series time, I visited with McCarthy to ask him who he liked in the upcoming confrontation. He never gave long-winded answers. He seldom identified the team. Instead, he named the league. Example: "I like the Nationals."

Why?

"Nobody in that other league knows how to throw a curve ball."

Joe McCarthy was an endearing man. Very private, but if you

were in his home, he made you feel welcome. He died in 1978 at age 90. I was privileged to be a pall bearer at his funeral.

TED WILLIAMS

I was a die-hard Ted Williams fan from the time he got into the major leagues in 1939.

Most of my pals were fans of Joe DiMaggio, a great player I respected, but he was a Yankee. There's a certain kinship between fans of the Brooklyn Dodgers and those of Williams's team, the Red Sox; in those days they shared the postseason sense of futility that came with never getting to the World Series. So it was easy for me, a Dodger fan, to back the Red Sox in the American League. Of course, this was long before the Dodgers abandoned Brooklyn for Los Angeles. That move has never been forgiven.

Williams's career is well documented by more perceptive writers than I, John Updike included. He was at Fenway Park the day Williams played his last game there and hit a homer in his last at-bat. Updike documented the event for the *New Yorker* magazine.

I did get to see Williams play when I was living in Hartford. The Sox were hosting the Cleveland Indians, who were employing the "Boudreau Shift" on Williams. Lou Boudreau, who once played for the Buffalo Bisons, was the playing manager of the Indians.

In the strategy devised to thwart Williams — a left-handed hitter who "always" pulled the ball — he moved the left outfielder over to right field to assist there, leaving only one player on the left side of the infield.

Bob Feller was on the mound for the Indians that day, and the ploy sometimes worked, but not all the time. Late in the game, Williams plunked a line-drive double to left, and nobody was there. The crowd went crazy. Williams drove in two runs and the Sox won. I loved it.

But the real thrill for me came years later, after Williams had retired to become a Hall of Fame fisherman. I was doing the sports desk at KB TV. Charlie Cox, who ran promotions for Sears, Roebuck in Buffalo, called one day to ask if I would like to interview Williams.

Most self-respecting sports reporters would never admit to excitement upon hearing that question. In this case, I had no self-respect; I was thrilled. It took me a desperate few seconds, but I was able to control myself and casually say, "Sure, Charlie. Can you be here by 5:30?"

"Here" was the Channel 7 studios on Main Street. The interview had little or nothing to do with baseball. It was about fishing and the new line of equipment Williams was endorsing and Sears was selling. After the show, I accompanied Charlie and Ted (an old pal by now) to a big downtown banquet.

Before the banquet got underway, a small group of VIPs was invited to meet Williams. Ted had left us to prepare for the event, so Charlie and I waited for him along with the rest. The room suddenly became quiet even before the door opened. Everyone knew Ted Williams was about to enter. There were no cues. His presence was just felt. He had that kind of aura about him.

Interviewing Bob Lanier. A great guy and really, really tall!

7
GAMES OF THE 1970S

NEW TEAMS IN TOWN

Nineteen-seventy was a big year for professional sports in Western New York. It was the year both the Buffalo Sabres and the Buffalo Braves took up residence at Memorial Auditorium. The Sabres are still a big part of the sports scene in Western New York. The Braves, sadly, are not. Both had interesting beginnings, going through several twists and turns before beginning operations.

I'll talk later about the Sabres, but first the Braves. It was the late 1960s when I got a call from Eddie Donovan, then general manager of the New York Knicks and formerly the basketball coach at St. Bonaventure.

The first thing he said to me was, "I never made this call."

"I've forgotten it already," I said. It was obvious that the GM of the Knicks wouldn't want anyone to know he was making such a call. He asked if I thought a pro basketball team would do well in Buffalo. After my emphatic "YES," he confided that the Cincinnati Royals were going up for sale. Would any investors be interested in moving the team to Buffalo? And what dates would be available at the Aud? None of this was public knowledge at the time. I surmised that Donovan had a strong interest in being part of an NBA franchise in Buffalo.

I assured him that I would look into the matter and get back to him. I called my friend Leonard Rochwarger, chairman of Firstmark Corp. in Buffalo and a rabid basketball fan. I asked if he thought a group of investors could be assembled. He answered enthusiastically in the affirmative. But there was one problem. The owners of the Royals also owned the Cincinnati Gardens, where the team played, so purchase of the Gardens would have to be part of the deal. There was no interest in owning the arena in Cincinnati if the team was going to move to Buffalo.

Logical, I'd say; end of investigation. I let Eddie know. Not long after, Eddie made another "non-call." The news was that the NBA was going to expand, and Buffalo was a target. The fight over who would get the franchise is well documented, so there is no reason for a recap, but I got a bit of a scoop from developer Paul Snyder. He tipped me off that he was going to buy the franchise, but said I couldn't use the information. I told him not to tell me. He insisted on telling me, and I kept his secret, but not for long.

The Braves put together a very competitive team thanks to the work of Donovan, who left the Knicks to become the Braves'

Interviewing Braves GM Eddie Donovan. The former NY Knicks GM built a quick contender in Buffalo.

Interviewing Niagara University basketball star and St. Joe's product Phil Scaffidi during a St. Bonaventure game broadcast. I believe Scaffidi was the finest all-around athlete to come from Western New York. His bright career ended far too early when he succumbed to cancer in 1980.

first GM. By the time he had drafted players like Bob McAdoo, Ernie DiGregorio, and Randy Smith — and finally got a coach like Jack Ramsay — they were good enough to go head to head with the Celtics and the Knicks, and got to the playoffs. They were a team that was fun to watch. But Ramsay was fired after the 1975–1976 season. The team lost in the playoffs against the Celtics in '76, and it was all downhill for the franchise after that.

For a definitive history of the Braves, I suggest Tim and Chris Wendel's superb book, *Buffalo, Home of the Braves*. A labor of love, it is full of pictures and information, including a run of articles by my old pal Phil Ranallo, probably the Braves' number one fan.

THE LITTLE THREE GOES BIG TIME

A ton of terrific basketball players bounced the ball for area colleges through the years playing in what was called the "Little Three" (Canisius College, Niagara University, and St. Bonaventure) and at the University at Buffalo and Buffalo State University. It's a long list and in trying to name them all, I'd be sure to leave out a few who deserved to be there; I'd be a bum for forgetting some and probably start a few arguments leading to fisticuffs.

But here goes anyway: A notch above the rest would be Calvin Murphy of Niagara, Bob Lanier of St. Bonaventure, Randy Smith of Buffalo State, John McCarthy and Bob MacKinnon of Canisius, and Jim Horne of UB.

Many from the "Little Three" went on to distinguished careers in the NBA. Calvin led the nation in scoring, and in a game of giants he never touched the five-foot-ten mark.

In contrast, Lanier was six-eleven. Both he and Murphy played in several postseason tournaments, and Lanier and the Bonnies made it to the NCAA Final Four in 1970. It was one of the years that Channel 7 carried a series of Bonaventure games. At one point they were ranked as high as No. 3 in the nation. That Bona team was loaded and Lanier was the go-to guy. But he didn't play in the Final Four, and they lost to Jacksonville, a team led by Artis Gilmore, who went on to become a star in both the ABA and the NBA.

What a matchup that would have been. Lanier had injured a knee in the game prior to the Final Four and never got a chance to go head-to-head with Gilmore. He was back in a Buffalo hospital watching the game, and I was visiting. Nobody else was there. We rooted hard and both felt that the Bonnies just might have been national champs had Lanier been able to play.

BOWLING IN BUFFALO

There's not much left of professional bowling in Buffalo, or elsewhere. But there was a heyday, from the 1950s, '60s, and peaking in the '70s.

At one time bowling shows were all over television, nationally and locally. The best-known local show was *Beat the Champ*, hosted by Chuck Healy on Channel 4. You don't see that kind of thing much anymore. Sad really, because amateur leagues benefited from the exposure. There were pro leagues too, and Western New York and the city had a slew of them that were nationally ranked. Even my employer got into the act; the Channel 7 team bowled in the American Bowling Congress championships in 1963. I choose to forget how we did (not well). I'll blame that lapse on age.

Tom Baker, who hailed from the Riverside neighborhood of Buffalo, is in the Professional Bowlers Association Hall of Fame. So is Lockport native Allie Brandt, who once bowled 886 for a three-game series, a professional record that stood for fifty years. A popular bowling center is named for him in his hometown. The late Anthony "Nin" Angelo kept local fans pinned to their TVs as he won *Beat the Champ* nineteen weeks in a row. His son Brad became a pro, and distinguished himself with two PBA tour titles.

Other local notables included Jim Schroeder, Gordie McMahon, Chet Mazur, Frank and Joe Caruana, Al LaCrego, Dick Ciprich, Phyllis Notaro, Doris and Cindy Coburn, and Art Jeziorski — and that's just a few.

TENNIS IN BUFFALO

The number of tennis emporiums in Western New York exploded during the 1960s and '70s. Everyone was playing, including my wife and me. It produced many good players, and some outstanding ones. The top two, in my humble opinion, were Jimmy Arias and Bobby Banck. Both are in the Greater Buffalo Sports Hall of Fame. Both joined the pro tour, and Arias won close to $2 million in four tour championships. Among the numerous local amateur players of note were the Reverend Bob Hetherington, Charlie Garfinkle, and Van Miller, who played almost daily.

I remember a doubles match between Arias and Banck and Miller and me. I was a misfit, but I enjoyed every minute of it. I asked Banck recently if he remembered, and he swore that he did. Both he and Arias are still in the tennis business and are no doubt enjoying every minute of it. They both brought much positive attention to Buffalo and Western New York.

Two other notable athletes in the area weren't tennis players, but they did play with racquets. Ethel Marshall and Bea Massman owned the badminton courts. Both were born and raised in Buffalo and became world-renowned in their sport. They were both pretty good tennis players as well, winning numerous area titles and coaching tennis along with badminton. I was pleased to help vote them into the Greater Buffalo Sports Hall of Fame in 1991.

CHAPTER 7

ARTHUR ASHE

At least eight books have been written about Arthur Ashe, another four were written by him ... and the subjects of all of them were tennis and social justice.

Ashe was a finalist in six Grand Slam singles championships, winning three times. He was also in five Grand Slam doubles championships, winning twice. The stadium in New York City where the US Open is played is named in his honor.

Ashe was a no-nonsense guy both on and off the court. Those who've seen him play saw a countenance that never changed expression. Determination was his constant companion. He was arrested twice, once for protesting against apartheid in South Africa, and once during a protest at the White House against a crackdown on Haitian refugees.

I had the privilege of interviewing Ashe in 1974 when Buffalo was represented in World Team Tennis. The conversation led naturally to the involvement of black athletes in the sport. I asked him if he was encouraging young African-Americans to consider tennis rather than football or basketball or baseball.

"No," he answered rather emphatically. "I'm encouraging them to consider becoming doctors or lawyers or engineers."

He taught me a great lesson that I have not forgotten to this day: never assume anything.

On the ice for the first puck drop of the Buffalo Sabres in 1970. Floyd Smith is on the left for the Sabres and Jean Béliveau on the right for the Canadiens.

8
ON THE ICE

THE BUFFALO SABRES

The other team that came into existence in 1970 was the Buffalo Sabres, and happily, they are still in business. It took some doing by the Knox brothers, Seymour III and Northrup, scions of one of Buffalo's most storied families and themselves natural athletes.

The tale actually begins with another set of brothers — Al, Sam, and Ruby Pastor. They owned the Buffalo Bison AHL hockey team and the local Pepsi-Cola distributorship. I'm not sure any of them were athletes. They were from the Bronx, so perhaps, like me, they played stickball on the streets of New York when they were kids. The Pastors bought the Bisons in 1957, and in 1966 they had a meeting with the Knox brothers. A coalition was formed to apply for an NHL franchise. The NHL had decided it was time to expand; if it didn't, the Western Hockey league was going to declare itself a major league and would be competing directly with the NHL for lucrative television contracts. The NHL added six teams to its roster of the so-called "Original Six" teams from Boston, Chicago, Detroit, Montreal, New York

City, and Toronto. The Knox brothers, with support from the Pastors, jumped at the chance to bring the NHL to Buffalo.

Therein starts the muddle. The AHL Bisons had agreed to be a farm team to both the Detroit Red Wings and the New York Rangers. Detroit and the Chicago Blackhawks were controlled by the Norris family of Chicago at the time. The Pastors had some problems with the Red Wings holding up their end of the arrangement — they didn't send down the specified number of players, for example — so the Pastors dealt mostly with the Rangers. Apparently, Bruce Norris, then owner of the Red Wings and a member of the NHL board of governors, did not appreciate the Pastors' tactics. The Norrises — Bruce and his half-brother James, who owned the Blackhawks — then blocked the Knoxes' expansion application because the Pastors were involved. Get-even time, I guess.

When the Knox application was denied, a new team went to St. Louis instead. St. Louis didn't have an ownership group that made an application, but it was awarded the franchise anyway. Why? James Norris owned the St. Louis Arena and needed a tenant.

The 1967 NHL expansion included a team that had previously been in the WHL, the San Francisco Seals, eventually renamed the California Golden Seals. Also added were the Los Angeles

Kings and the Minnesota North Stars. The original six teams howled, wanting more teams in the East, apparently to minimize travel time and expense. So Philadelphia and Pittsburgh were added along with the nonapplicant, St. Louis.

The NHL now had twelve teams, but was soon to expand again.

The Knox Brothers were far from out. They were a couple of smart fellows who could find their way around the most complicated maze ever designed, and the NHL at the time was indeed a complicated maze.

After being shut out in 1967, they bought a minority interest in the struggling California Golden Seals in 1969, intending to move the team to Buffalo. At the same time, the purchase gave them some maneuvering room on the NHL board of governors, putting them in a better position to do battle with the Norris clan. When expansion came up again in 1970, they gave up their interest in the Seals, and Buffalo and Vancouver were finally added to the fraternity. The AHL Bisons ceased operations after the 1969–1970 season; the Pastors did not stand in the way of the Knoxes and their new NHL team.

The young franchises held together even when the World Hockey Association was founded in 1972. The WHA only lasted until 1979, but during that time raised the salary bar while luring such stars as the Black Hawks' Bobby Hull away from their teams. But the NHL got its act together and the WHA folded after seven years of war.

In the meantime, the Knox brothers were able to entice one of the sharpest hockey minds in the business, George "Punch" Imlach, to Buffalo. Imlach, who had guided Toronto to four Stanley Cups in six years before falling out of favor with Maple Leafs management, became the Sabres' first coach and general manager. As 1970 expansion teams, Buffalo and the Vancouver Canucks vied for first position in the draft. The NHL used a roulette wheel to determine who would gain the right to draft the top player. Luck was a lady that night: Imlach called the right number as the wheel spun. This great story is captured in Ross Brewitt's book, *A Spin of the Wheel: the Birth of the Buffalo Sabres.*

In addition to being lucky, Imlach made some smart moves. He chose as his first draft pick Gilbert Perreault, a star junior player from Quebec, and followed in '71 by selecting Rick Martin, a high-scoring winger from the Montreal Junior Canadiens. The Canucks took Jocelyn Guevremont third in that same draft, and he later ended up in Buffalo, too, via a trade. In the spring of '72, Imlach traded veteran player Eddie Shack for René Robert of

PHOTO: COURTESY BILL WIPPERT

Sabres founder Seymour Knox urging me to don a jersey on the occasion of my retirement from Channel 7. "Put it on!" he said.

PHOTO: STAFF ANNOUNCER ARCHIVES

Punch Imlach always had a hat on, even during interviews. I never met anyone who knew more about hockey.

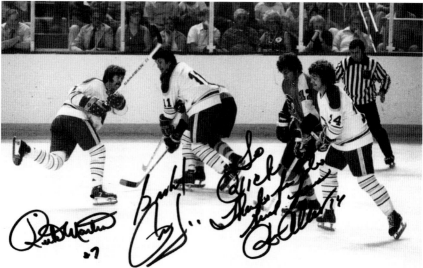

The French Connection: they liked to call me by my full name.

the Pittsburgh Penguins, and by '75, their fifth season, the team Imlach built was playing for the Stanley Cup. Unprecedented.

THE FRENCH CONNECTION

The French Connection was a popular movie when Imlach obtained Robert and new coach Joe Crozier teamed him with Martin and Perreault. The result was one of the most explosive, exciting lines ever to play in the NHL. Writers and broadcasters scampered frantically to come up with a tag for the fascinating things this trio was accomplishing on the ice. The one that stuck was "The French Connection." It was first heard on a 6:15 sportscast on Channel 7. Yes, my sportscast, but I can't take credit for it. Alan

Nesbitt, our assistant news director, and I were discussing the naming frenzy, and he suggested the movie title. It was a stroke of brilliance. I couldn't wait to lead with it. The lightbulbs in my brain were flashing like crazy. Paul Wieland, the Sabres PR man at the time, claimed it was first displayed on the message board at the Aud that same night. Could be, but the first time it was heard was on Channel 7, thanks to Alan Nesbitt.

The trio consistently led the Sabres to the Stanley Cup playoffs, always in spectacular fashion. Their accomplishments are too numerous to list here, and their popularity with fans is undiminished to this day. I remember running the same goal-scoring highlight, an end-to-end rush by Perreault, on my sportscast every night for a week. Perreault had a knack for such things, and this one was particularly noteworthy. I attended Sabres practices, and I recall Martin taking slap shots from the blue line, hitting the goal line marked on the boards opposite him, a diagonal shot across nearly half the rink. He'd hit the same spot almost every time. In games, Robert had an ability to be in the right place at the right time; he seemed to be able to anticipate what was about to unfold while he was on the ice. Fans, including me, couldn't get enough of these three. Amazing talents.

Not only were these men extremely entertaining, they were great friends and special people. René, the last to join the group, was not as outgoing as the other two. He was all business, both on and off the ice. He was the steadying force. But Martin and Perrault, off the ice, were colorful characters. They loved calling me by my real name — all six of my real names, that is.

I once asked Perreault what he would have been if not a hockey player. His answer: a rock and roll singer. Martin would have been a pro golfer. Sadly, he passed away unexpectedly in March 2011. After retiring, Robert entered the business world, and for a time was president of the NHL Alumni Association. In many ways, the gathering of these three individuals was a phenomenon. But to me, perhaps most memorable was their generosity with their time off the ice. They never refused me an interview, and I never saw them turn away a fan looking for an autograph.

What a thrill it was to watch those three play.

EXPENDABLE

As amazing as the French Connection was to reporters and fans alike, even the best players had difficultly staying in the good graces of the team's general manager. After all, hockey GMs could lose their jobs if the team didn't perform.

I remember having lunch with Imlach in 1976 after the Sabres had been knocked out of the playoffs early. The team had gone all the way to the Stanley Cup finals the year before. Imlach could put on a great bluster, but he loved his players, he loved his team. He also knew how to handle the media; he always had something clever to say. But the day we had lunch, he was upset. "I'll trade the whole lot of them," he threatened.

"You don't mean that," I said.

"Yes, I do," he replied.

I challenged him further. "You wouldn't trade Perreault, would you? Or Rick Martin? Or René Robert? Or Jim Schoenfeld? Or Danny Gare?" I went through the whole roster. He finally admitted he wouldn't. There were no trades, at least not that day.

Scotty Bowman, who was the Sabres GM from 1979 to 1987, had his own approach. In December 1981, he traded team captain Gare, defenseman Schoenfeld, and forward Derek Smith — all incredibly popular players with fans — to the Red Wings in exchange for forwards Mike Foligno and Dale McCourt, and right winger Brent Peterson. Later that same season he traded Martin to the Los Angeles Kings; he had already dealt Robert in 1979, breaking up the French Connection. You never knew what to expect with Bowman; it seemed like pretty much any player was expendable.

Jim Schoenfeld was a neighbor of mine when he played for the Sabres. When word of the trade got out, I went to his house to get his impressions, although I didn't interview him on camera. He said the right things: that he was looking forward to the change. But it was clear there was more that he wasn't telling me. The next day, the three former Sabres were leaving for Detroit. This was about as big a story as I can recall during my time as sports director. The whole town was mourning their departure, Schoenfeld and Gare in particular. At the airport, I interviewed Schoenfeld on camera, asking him if he felt any different about the trade than he had the day before. He paused and with tears coming to his eyes said, "All I can think about right now is that I'm not going to be home tonight to have dinner with my kids." Then he put his arm around my shoulder. He couldn't bring himself to say anything else. With those few words, Schoenfeld illustrated how connected he was to his family and the community, and that his departure was about more than the game he played. It was a great moment.

WAYNE GRETZKY

This tale is from February 1982. Wayne Gretzky and the Edmonton Oilers had come through Buffalo on an eastern road trip. Gretzky was tearing up the league (again), scoring goals and handing out assists at a pace faster than a cartoon roadrunner.

Wayne Gretzky signs autographs outside Sabreland in the Town of Wheatfield after a practice session in preparation for tonight's game

COURIER-EXPRESS/PAUL PASQUARELLO

between his Edmonton Oilers and the Buffalo Sabres, in which he will be seeking to break the single-season scoring record of 76 goals.

An Unpretentious Star Charms Fans

By Mike Billoni
COURIER EXPRESS STAFF REPORTER

for Time, patiently signed autographs for 20 minutes while his teammates waited in the team bus.

North Tonawanda grammar school class skating at the arena. As he made his way to the locker room, a youngster looked up and meek-

Wayne Gretzky caused quite a stir in 1981 when he set a new single-season goal-scoring record in Buffalo. He left town with a few autographs, as well.

He was on the brink of breaking Phil Esposito's single-season scoring record of seventy-six goals. The Oilers hung around for three days, one of which included a game against the Sabres. Gil Perreault had a hat trick in that game, but so did Gretzky, setting the new goal-scoring record.

Gretzky's presence drew a record crowd of fans and reporters at Oilers' practice sessions. Normally, the only people present would be the beat reporters who covered the team. But with all the attention on Gretzky, it turned into a mob scene, everyone wanting an exclusive one-on-one interview with the Great One, me included.

I saw that the big crowd would be a problem. I suggested to the Oilers PR guy that we turn it into a press conference, which would allow Gretzky to answer questions from everyone. He checked with Gretzky. The answer was yes.

A microphone was set up, but before going to it, Gretzky came directly over to me and said, "My mom said if I saw you to say hello because she watches you all the time." And he asked for my autograph.

Dumbfounded, I looked at Mike Billoni of the *Courier-Express* who was standing next to me, and said, "Can you believe what he said to me?" It took me a while to I realize that Gretzky grew up in Brantford, Ontario, a town that was within the signal reach of Channel 7. Apparently Mrs. Gretzky was a fan of Irv, Rick, and Tom.

He got Irv's and Tom's autograph, too.

DON CHERRY

Don Cherry, or "Grapes," as he is sometimes affectionately known (although, rumor has it, sometimes unaffectionately, too) was an almost-resident of Western New York, since his name adorns a popular chain of restaurants throughout Canada, one just over the border from Buffalo in Fort Erie, Canada.

It's impossible to fully characterize this man. Some call him a wacko, but he's not so wacko that he couldn't be voted the seventh "Greatest Canadian" by the Canadian Broadcasting Corporation. I don't know if his white bull terrier, Blue, was included.

Cherry has written books, acted in movies and on television, and says whatever is on his mind and doesn't care who hears it. His charitable work is monumental and he devotes a lot of time to it. He was also a hockey player and NHL coach: he played in one game for the Boston Bruins and coached the team for seven seasons. He also coached the Colorado Rockies for two seasons. He had a very successful career in the AHL before that, but he is most famous for his work since 1980 on CBC television. He is a living legend. The print guys either love him or hate him, but they always write about him.

I once did an interview with him, airing a minute or two of it on the 11 o'clock sports for five straight nights. Sample question: What do you think of the Sabres trading defenseman Larry Playfair? His answer: "You never trade tough guys. When that fancy-dancy winger comes down the ice and he sees that tough guy, the fancy-dancy guy says, 'Uh-oh,' and changes direction. You never trade tough guys."

At that time the Sabres were contemplating a change in coaches. I asked Cherry if he would ever get back into coaching. "Only two places I might go are Hamilton, if they ever got an NHL franchise," he replied, "and the other is Buffalo."

I suggested to Seymour Knox that he contact Don. "I don't think we could afford him," Knox said. He was probably right in more ways than one. That exchange took place in the early 1980s, and Don is still working in his late seventies. And I wouldn't bet against him still being at it ten or fifteen years from now. He's one of my favorite characters.

Blood and Ice

This is a serious story that might have had an unhappy ending. It doesn't.

A long time ago my father took me to a movie called *Blood and Sand*. It starred Tyrone Power — a big leading man then — as a matador in Spain. I think my father always dreamed of becoming a matador, as did probably every other boy in Spain. The advertising on the movie poster showed blood spattered on the sand of the arena, or *plaza de toros*. The bull usually loses, but not always. The blood on the sand might belong to a gored bull fighter.

I was reminded of that scene on the evening of March 22, 1989, three months before I retired. I was at Memorial Auditorium catching the first period of a game between the Sabres and the St. Louis Blues. Suddenly there was blood on the ice after a collision in front of Sabres goalie Clint Malarchuk. It was Malarchuk's blood, gushing from his neck after being slashed by the skate of Steve Tuttle, a Blues winger.

It was a horrific scene. People were screaming; many fainted. Many in the arena thought Malarchuk was going to die. And he might have, but for the presence of mind of Jim Pizzutelli, the Sabres trainer. Jim rushed onto the ice, desperately trying not to slip. When he got to Malarchuk, he seemed to stick his entire fist into the goalie's neck.

Malarchuk did not die, but he needed more than 300 stitches to close the wound. Had Tuttle's skate struck Malarchuk just a fraction of an inch higher, the outcome would have been very different. He soon resumed his playing career and later coached. The next day in an interview with Pizzutelli, I asked him how he knew exactly what to do.

"I served in Vietnam and saw stuff like this all the time," he said. "I knew what blood vessel I needed to pinch in order to stop the bleeding." His quick action saved Clint's life.

Like matadors, professional hockey players, football players, and all those involved in contact sports risk their lives when they step onto their field of play. The consequences may become spectacle for some. We showed much of Jim's actions on our broadcast, but we never showed the blood on the ice.

Do You Believe in Miracles?

ABC-TV announcer Al Michaels famously uttered those words when the United States National Hockey Team defeated the Soviet Union National Team at the 1980 Winter Olympics at Lake Placid. Team USA went on to beat Finland for the gold medal. It truly was a miracle, since the Soviets had been a powerhouse for many decades preceding those games, and the US team was made up of a bunch of college kids and amateurs. Channel 7 had sent me to Lake Placid to cover the games. I had a chance to interview a young defenseman on the US team, and later I witnessed the miracle — both the win over the Soviets and the gold medal victory against the Finns.

Big games and championships tend to make fans of us all, but in 1980, the Winter Games did not command the same attention from US audiences that they do now. Today, media coverage is total. Networks pay big bucks for the broadcast rights, and the

My press pass for the gold medal game, Team USA vs. Finland in the 1980 Winter Olympics. A simpler time.

public is saturated with all things Olympic. Only 8,500 people saw the US defeat the Soviets; now huge stadiums are constructed for all Olympic games, and the broadcasts show every angle, every moment.

In 1988, the Olympics began allowing professional athletes to compete in the games, and starting in 1998, the NHL permitted their players to participate. It's hard to imagine that the US will ever again field a team of no-names like they did in 1980; it's professionals only now.

It may be a stretch to say that Al Michaels understood how the games would change when he made his famous declaration. But his words are forever connected to one of the greatest accomplishments in team sports, one that is unlikely to be repeated.

The young player I interviewed? It was Mike Ramsey, an outstanding defenseman who, post-Olympic experience, played for the Buffalo Sabres for fourteen years and later became assistant coach. I was privileged to see him help win the gold for the USA.

To My Pal, Rick,
Mgr. Kelliher

The "Masked Marvel." In addition to being a man of the cloth, Monsignor Kelliher was one of the toughest guys I ever met.

9
FIGHTERS

THE MASKED MONSIGNOR

I was weaned on the likes of Joe Louis and Billy Conn in my early years in Brooklyn, but my first years in Buffalo were connected to guys like Lee Oma, a long-tenured Buffalo fighter who challenged Ezzard Charles for the heavyweight boxing title in 1951.

Western New York has a rich history in the boxing world, having been the home of such stellar performers as Jimmy Goodrich, Jimmy Slattery, Rocky Kansas, Tommy Paul, Joe and Phil Muscato, Henry Brimm, Joey Giambra, Jimmy Ralston, Vinny Cala, Bobby Scanlon, Joey DeJohn, Jackie Donnelly, Joe Matisi, Rocky Cudney, Vic Brown, and Jackie Donovan. I knew a few of those guys; most recently, Joe Mesi.

It's a long list, and you can check out boxing's background in Buffalo by getting connected with the Veteran Boxers Association. The local chapter is called Ring 44, and at this writing is headed by Jack Green.

All the names mentioned here and many more are members of the

Ring 44 Hall of Fame. Another member is Monsignor Franklin Kelliher. He was a boxer, a wrestler, and one of the toughest guys I ever knew. For many years he ran the Working Boys' Home on Vermont Street, a place for wayward young men found in the streets, who were perhaps lost in more ways than one. You had to be tougher than tough to run a place like that, and Kelliher was. He wrestled professionally under the name "Masked Marvel," until the bishop put a stop to it when he found out the Masked Marvel was also saying Mass on Sunday mornings.

I met him when he said Mass at St. Louis Church, where I was an altar boy. He helped our ragtag grammar school baseball team by providing us with some bats and balls, and even a couple of gloves. The monsignor also was responsible for the Golden Gloves boxing championship tournament staying alive for many years in Western New York after the *Courier-Express* dropped its sponsorship.

Money gained there went to keeping the Working Boys' Home from going under. The monsignor once caught a couple of toughs trying to burglarize his home in Ridgeway, Ontario. He decked them both before the police showed up.

He loved cooking lobster, as long as you brought the lobster. I last visited with him shortly before his death in 1985. He was a very special person and a long-time friend.

ALI

On a few occasions I found a way to interview Muhammad Ali. They mostly resulted in the normal hum-drum stuff in which the interviewer doesn't ask any insightful questions and the interviewee doesn't say anything memorable. But once something meaningful happened.

A local photographer called to ask if I would go to Toronto with him to interview Ali and George Chuvalo for ABC. It was March 1966, when Ali was in trouble with the US government. He objected to the Vietnam War and later refused to be drafted. Political opposition, including threatened boycotts by veterans' groups, forced him to scrap a scheduled title defense in Chicago and instead head to Maple Leaf Gardens for a bout with Chuvalo, the Canadian champion.

Our interview was about a week before the fight, which was scheduled for March 29. I accepted the invitation with the stipulation that I would have access to the tape of the interview and any other film taken that day. We started by attending a public workout that Ali charged everyone a buck to get into.

The workout included the expected: a punching bag, a couple rounds of sparring, and so forth. Several hundred people were there, including Jimmy Cannon, a boxing guru who had worked for the *New York Daily News*, the *New York Post*, and the *New York Journal-American*. (Not at the same time, of course.)

After Ali finished sparring, he invited members of the media to come up into the ring to be introduced. There were no takers until I jumped up and climbed into the ring. He introduced me (although he had forgotten our previous encounters). He then acknowledged Cannon, but Cannon wouldn't come up. Instead he said, "You do your fighting in the ring. I'll do mine out here."

Ali was not happy and responded, "It's guys like you who have kept me from fighting in my own country."

That was a clue for me. When I got back to my seat, I told the photographer to get to the dressing room right away. Ali spent another five minutes on the bag and then came into the dressing room and sat down next to me. We were about to start the interview when Cannon stormed into the room and faced off with Ali, almost nose-to-nose.

"Who's keeping you from fighting?" Cannon asked. "Not me!" And the shouting match began.

I motioned to the photographer to shoot what was happening. He refused because the network wanted footage of an interview.

Cannon continued, and Ali was shouting back. "There are people burning their draft cards in the US! Know where mine is? In my back pocket!" And with that he stormed off into another room.

If the encounter had been filmed, the photographer might have won an award, given Ali's notoriety.

As it was, when I interviewed Ali later, I had some juicy questions to ask about Cannon. It was obvious they didn't like each other. I asked Ali why. He said Cannon had berated him for his opposition to the war without ever asking the heavyweight champion about his position. They never made up. Ali did show me his draft card.

Ali was like no one I had ever talked to. He was always the center of attention. He saw to it that he was.

ROCKY MARCIANO

From the time I was eight years old, I was a fan of Joe Louis.

Why? Because my father was.

There was no TV in those days, so we listened to the boxing matches on the radio: Don Dunphy at his best. Joe Louis meant so much to so many people. He was a great champion, but he was also a humble and sincere person. Almost all of his fights were memorable, but it got to the point where few challengers were

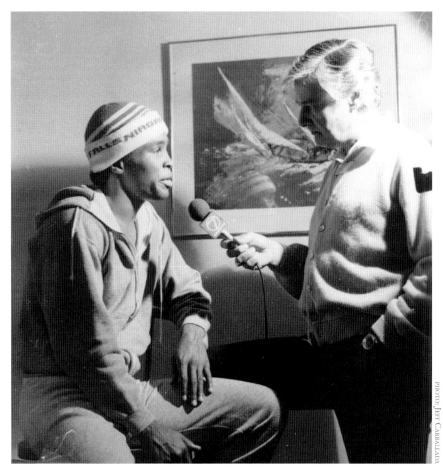

Interviewing Sugar Ray Leonard before a bout in Buffalo that never took place. Leonard was discovered to have a detached retina, and his May 1982 fight against Roger Stafford was canceled.

left except members of the so-called Bum of the Month Club.

He retired a champion, but as so many boxers do, attempted a comeback, apparently after getting into trouble with the Internal Revenue Service. After a series of victories, he faced an unbeaten young contender named Rocky Marciano, another humble and sincere person and a great champion. Rocky KO'd Louis.

Well after Rocky's retirement in 1956, he was in Buffalo and came to our studio for an interview. The conversation got around to his knockout of the great Joe Louis, who, at the time of their fight, was 37, nine years older than Rocky.

I saw that fight on TV and lamented, as so many others did, the sight of the great Joe Louis falling through the ropes.

"It was an emotional moment for me," I said to Rocky.

"It was for me, too," he said. "I loved Joe Louis. He was an inspiration to me. I wanted to be a champion like him. Seeing him go down wasn't a jubilant moment. I wanted to help him up."

His response said so much about who he was.

Nobody — nobody — ever beat Rocky Marciano. He retired undefeated. He was a delightful guy and by the end of our interview, I felt as though I had made a friend for life. I doubt he remembered me as much as I still remember him. The guy had soul.

FLOYD PATTERSON

"Were you a good kid or a bad kid when you were growing up?"

That was the first question I asked former heavyweight champion Floyd Patterson during his visit to Buffalo to fight Vic Brown in August 1971.

"I wasn't a bad kid," he said, "but I wasn't a good kid either. I was bad enough to be sent away to a special school when I was ten years old. It changed my life."

How?

"I never took part in class," he replied. "I sat in the last row feeling sorry for myself. Every Friday the teacher would ask a question and whoever knew the answer would get a bag of candy. I never knew the answer. One day she asked a question, and I knew the answer, but I didn't raise my hand. I was afraid I'd be wrong and they would laugh at me. Nobody else knew the answer and when the teacher gave the answer, I was right. I was so upset, I ran out of the room crying. The teacher ran after me, put her hand on my shoulder and said to me, 'Floyd, I know you knew the answer. I'm giving you the bag of candy.' That moment changed my whole life. That and the fact that it was at that school that I learned how to box."

Patterson became very good at boxing. He won an Olympic gold medal and had sixty-four fights as a professional, winning fifty-five of them. He won the heavyweight title by beating Archie Moore in five rounds in 1956 to become the youngest title-holder ever at the age of twenty-one.

I happened on my favorite story involving Patterson when I asked him if he ever hated a man in the ring. To my surprise he said yes: Ingemar Johansson.

The two had met in 1959, and Johansson had won the title with a third-round KO. Apparently he mouthed off a lot about his victory, deriding Patterson's abilities and his race. "I hated him for that," Patterson told me.

In the 1960 rematch, Patterson KO'd Johansson in the sixth round, making him the first boxer to regain the heavyweight championship.

"I stood over him after he hit the canvas hard," he said, "watching his left leg shaking, and I really got scared. Why did I hate this man so much? He lay unconscious, and I knelt down to hold him while his handlers were scrambling to get into the ring."

The two met once again a year later with Patterson winning the rubber. They then became lifelong friends, taking turns visiting each other in their home countries.

THE ONION FARMER

We have already talked about Louis, Ali, Marciano, Patterson, and

With Carmen Basilio: I was lucky to be friends with this very tough guy.

Another successful tournament on the DiPaolo bocce courts, 1994.
From left: Mike Toppo, Michael DiPaolo, Bob Dingwall, Bob Koshinski,
Dennis DiPaolo, Dennis' son Ilio, myself, Ilio DiPaolo, Bob Stotz.

several of the local guys, but I never had a chance to play golf with any of them. I did, however, have the pleasure of hitting the links with another champion, Carmen Basilio, the onion farmer from Canastota, New York, and one of the great characters of all time.

Basilio had seventy-nine fights. The first one was in November 1948, and he had fought four times by the end of that year. In his career, he won fifty-six of those seventy-nine fights, forty-seven by a KO. He lost sixteen and drew seven. He was a regular in the heyday of televised boxing. Friday night fights were a weekly attraction, and Basilio was in the mix along with guys like Chuck Davey, Lew Jenkins, Kid Gavilan, and Sugar Ray Robinson.

The 1950s were All-Star time in the boxing world. Basilio won his first title in June 1955 with a twelfth-round KO of Tony DeMarco. He retained the title in a rematch that November. Basilio and Johnny Saxton traded wins in 1956, and a year later Basilio won the middleweight title with a fifteen-round split decision over Sugar Ray Robinson. Sugar Ray won it back with a controversial split decision in March 1958.

I love the story Basilio told about Jake LaMotta and Rocky Graziano leaving a casino in Las Vegas in the early morning hours, the sun just coming up.

"Is that the sun or the moon up there?" Jake asks.

"I don't know, Jake," Rocky says. "I'm not from around here."

Boxers are a breed of their own. I asked Basilio if he remembered a fight he had with DeMarco when his knees buckled in the fifth round but he didn't hit the canvas.

"Remember it? I was there."

I never had an ill word with Carmen Basilio, the onion farmer from Canastota. Sadly, he passed away in November 2012.

He never did like Sugar Ray.

ILIO DIPAOLO

How does one describe a person who had such immense charisma to go along with his equally Bunyanesque physique?

Ilio DiPaolo's professional career as a wrestler is well documented. He was a champion, after all, and champions have a peculiar way of becoming well known. But this is not a tale of his professional accomplishments. This is a description of a man whose heart and soul were bigger than his considerable frame. That is what DiPaolo was and still is in the minds of those who knew him.

Who knows how he came to be the way he was. As a youngster in Introdacqua, Italy, he was struck with polio. Determined to conquer that awful disease, DiPaolo took up what we Americans know as soccer to strengthen his legs. This hardship so early in his life may have been the catalyst that produced one of the most caring persons it has been my privilege to know.

DiPaolo entertained many as a wrestler in the 1950s and '60s. Later, he opened a restaurant and, with wonderful food and his gregarious nature, he continued to deliver enjoyment to all who came to see him. He used his success to give back to the community at every opportunity.

There is an entire generation in Western New York who know little of Ilio's wrestling career, but they know the enormity of the person. His generosity and graciousness are legendary. What he has done for others would fill another book. Ask any Bills player, many of whom spent hours in his well-known restaurant, now run by his sons Dennis and Michael. Or the many high school athletes and their parents who have dined there on special occasions. Or other former wrestlers such as Dick the Destroyer. Carmen Basilio would have told you the same thing. None of them would remark on what a great wrestler DiPaolo was; they'd talk about what a special person he was.

He would arrange a bocce tournament at his home or at the restaurant at the drop of a hat. He hosted a yearly tournament for the workers at Channel 7 and for the Bills and for who knows how many others.

The sad thing is that we have to use the word was. DiPaolo was struck by a car on a rainy afternoon in 1995 and died at the age of 69. But his family sees to it that the traditions continue, and the food is still as good as ever.

Arnold Palmer practicing his putts at the 1980 PGA Championship
at Oak Hill in Rochester.

10
HITTING THE LINKS

GOLF IN WESTERN NEW YORK

Many now-famous pro golfers played in Western New York at a young age. Let's start with Phil Mickelson and Tiger Woods. Who's more famous than that?

Add to the list Jim Furyk, Steve Stricker, Jeff Maggert, Kenny Perry, Jeff Sluman, Bob Tway, Corey Pavin, Hunter Mahan, Rocco Mediate, Mark Brooks, Jay Haas, Mark O'Meara, Matt Kuchar, Tom Lehman, Davis Love, Anthony Kim, and dozens of others including Fred Couples, my wife's favorite. She calls him "Cutie Pie," having once carried a divot of his in a paper cup during a Ryder Cup match at Oak Hill.

Many local players made headlines, as well: Ward Wettlaufer, John Konsek, Lancy Smith (who captained the women's Curtis Cup team), Cookie Berger, E. J. Pfister, Tim Straub, Fred Silver, Allen and Cindy Miller, Patty Jordon, Kim Kaul, Don Allen, and more.

A long list of greats, and they all played at the Niagara Falls

Country Club. They were not pros then, but played as amateurs in the Porter Cup Championship.

Jack Nicklaus's son, Gary, played there. So did Bing Crosby's son, Nathaniel, and Guy Boros, the son of Julius Boros, who won three major championships. This is how important an event the Porter Cup has been and continues to be. We often take local events for granted, but we shouldn't.

Pro Golfers

Being a hacker does not preclude one from being a fan. Even if you're a sports reporter, it's difficult not to be amazed at just how good pro golfers are at their trade — which doesn't mean you have to like them. Most are pretty nice guys, just as in any other pro sport. Some are dips, others rude, some cold and indifferent, but most are OK. There will be no who's who list here, only some tidbits about several whom I came to know as a sportscaster.

Believe it or not, my first interview with a professional golfer was with Arnold Palmer. Cross my heart. Said heart was pumping out of control, but I couldn't have been luckier. He immediately set me at ease; he's that kind of guy. Easily and candidly, he explained how he had lost an Open championship to Billy Casper. Years later, at Oakmont, I had scheduled an interview at the eighteenth green right after a practice round. He got to me, but not before he encouraged a cute little six-year-old girl to get his autograph. He is a born charmer.

Once, Edith, our then 15-year-old son, Jeff, and I spent three days at Bay Hill, Palmer's golf course outside Orlando. Palmer's pal Dow Finsterwald was also there, and we shared a few libations together. Palmer spent a big part of his mornings tinkering with golf clubs. His garage did not house an automobile, but it did sport perhaps five hundred clubs — every make, number, and swing shaft. Putters, too. I wandered down there one morning and we had a great chat about them.

At dinner, he made sure to take the time to visit our table, introduce us to his wife, and send over an after-dinner drink.

Jack Nicklaus was a totally different personality, at least with the public. I interviewed him many times, too, but there weren't many laughs; he maintained a serious demeanor except when he talked about his kids, who were trying to become pro golfers, too, with little success (his son, Gary, did win the Porter Cup in 1991). But for the most part, it was strictly business with Jack.

With Lee Trevino, what you see is what you get. He is approachable, animated, and jokes all the time. I asked him once about his practice routine. He said he always goes to the practice tee to talk to his pals. Maybe he didn't want to mess with his

With Jack Nicklaus at the Canadian Open. He was all business.

I played a few rounds with Jim Thorpe. He taught me how a pro golfer
approaches the game.

swing. Nicklaus said Trevino was the best ball striker he had ever observed.

Greg Norman was hitting 300-plus drives in the mid-1980s with a persimmon-wood club. He answered my question on how he eagled the 500-plus-yard eighteenth hole at Glen Abbey by saying, "I hit a driver, then a nine-iron. It was a balata [soft] ball, too." But many of the players in those days were doing the same thing. It makes me wonder what they could have done with today's metal clubs and rock-hard golf balls. Just asking.

JIM THORPE

On a June 1981 afternoon, I was making my usual visits to the Teletype sports wire in preparation for my show, when I noticed that a guy named Jim Thorpe was among the leaders of the US Open. His hometown was listed as Buffalo, but I had never heard of him. Several pro golfers lived in Western New York, but none were on the pro tour, much less a challenger in the US Open. I immediately called some of the local pros to inquire if they knew this guy.

The answer I got was that he had recently moved to Western New York after marrying a Buffalo gal. Eventually, I interviewed him, which led to a budding friendship, and several rounds of golf. Intimidating golf, but it taught me how a pro golfer's mind works.

We were teeing off at the first hole at Brookfield Country Club in Clarence, where I was a member. It's a long par-four from the championship tees, or "tips." Pros always play from the tips. Hackers like me seldom if ever play from the tips, except when you play with a pro.

I hit a solid drive down the middle and used a six iron for my second shot. Thorpe blasted his drive and hit a wedge for his approach. I was about to learn something. The pin was located in the back left of the green. I went for the middle of the green. He went right at the stick.

His ball landed close to the pin but took an erratic bounce and dropped off the back edge and down a slope. I asked him why he played that shot, instead of playing it safe like me.

"I'd always play that shot," he said. "Today, it bounced off the green. Tomorrow, it might stay right next to the pin. If you can't handle that, don't play this game."

Although he didn't win the Open, Thorpe earned three PGA tour wins, won the Canadian PGA Championship in 1982, and went on to have great success on the Champions Tour for pros over the age of fifty. Moreover, he taught me a great lesson about the game of golf.

PORTER CUP 1982

In the summer of 1981, the New York State Amateur Golf Association held its annual championship at the Wanakah Country Club, which says plenty about the quality of golf courses in Western New York.

One of the participants was a local college kid who attended Stanford University. As we chatted, I mentioned that I would probably see him at the upcoming Porter Cup Championship, one of the most prestigious amateur contests in the country. People like Tiger and Phil and recent US Open title-holder Webb Simpson participated in it every year.

I was surprised to learn that this young player had not been invited to play in the Porter Cup. "No matter," I said. "You can get in by playing in the qualifier."

But there was a catch: the local qualifier round no longer existed, he said. I was dumbfounded. That meant that none of the locals with a handicap of two or better would have a chance to play. Many superb players in Western New York and southern Ontario had qualified in the past, but now were being shut out. I couldn't believe it, and decided that an injustice had been done.

I called to verify the cancellation and did a commentary on the six o'clock news pointing out the error of this policy.

A sidebar to this, and one that I took into consideration before sticking my neck out, was the fact that I had played a lot of golf (badly) at the Niagara Falls Country Club. My in-laws were members there. I knew the pro and most members of the committee promoting the event. The chairman, Dr. William McMahon, had been a guest at our wedding. So I had many reasons to reconsider. But I did not change my mind and went ahead with the commentary.

Well, the you-know-what hit the fan. I received a scathing letter from Dr. McMahon telling me to mind my own business and to leave the editorializing to my boss. But he also gave me an out. He wrote: "If you can get us a good enough golf course to host the qualifier, we might reconsider."

I picked up the phone, called one of the owners of Glen Oak in East Amherst — a course designed by golf great Robert Trent Jones — and read him the letter. Without hesitation, he said, "No problem. Glad to do it."

I relayed the message, and Dr. McMahon had no recourse; the qualifier was back on. NFCC continues to hold the tournament, now on its own course.

My name was mud at NFCC for some time, and I felt for my in-laws, but they handled it. A year later, when I showed up at the annual press luncheon, Dr. McMahon, still in charge, sat at my table. Without mentioning my name, he thanked the "member of the media" who pointed out the error of their ways regarding the local qualifier.

"Buffalo: the city that is not so big...and not so small. It's in the comfort zone."

11
MY CITY

GBSHOF

This is the acronym of the Greater Buffalo Sports Hall of Fame.

I'm happy to say that this is now a permanent part of the fabric of the Buffalo sports scene, and the induction ceremony is much anticipated every fall.

About a year after I left Channel 7, longtime pal Lars Hjalmquist, a successful businessman, asked me to join him in a new venture. He had a successful home healthcare business and several other smaller companies working out of his office on Sheridan Drive in Tonawanda. He wanted to start another company with me. We made a deal, and so began Rick Azar Associates, a marketing and public relations firm.

One day at the office I got a call from someone named John Kapelewski, an insurance executive who had just transferred to Buffalo from Central New York. The call had nothing to do with insurance; instead, he wanted me to join him in an effort to start a local Sports Hall of Fame, as he had done successfully in

Receiving the honor of being inducted into the Greater Buffalo Sports Hall of Fame in 1997. I never would have gotten this without the help of my pals.

Syracuse. I didn't think much of the idea and tried hard to beg out of it, but, like most insurance guys, John didn't give up. I finally agreed to meet with him, never dreaming how successful this venture would eventually become.

Some twenty-five people were initially involved, ten of whom remain. People like Tim McGrath, president of Personal Computers, Inc.; attorney Bill Crowe; former Bills' great Booker Edgerson; attorney Warren Gelman; former Bills' team doctor Ed Gicewicz; physician Dave Myers; developer Jim Tzetzo; educator and coach Sister Maria Pares; and businessman Steve Ulmer.

Many others have supported the venture on and off through the years, but the board has been, for the most part, a bunch of hard-working, interested, and concerned people. It wasn't easy in the early days, and it isn't easy now. It takes a dedicated crew, none of whom have ever been paid for their efforts. I can't say enough about them, especially the initial officers, Kap (Kapelewski), Sister Maria, McGrath, and Crowe.

We tried to get the *Buffalo News* involved initially, but the effort was greeted with skepticism. They sent a reporter, the late Jim Kelley, to inquire about our efforts. He was a friend, but you'd never know it. He did his job, as he should have, and asked me some tough questions. To this day, I'm not sure he was convinced it was a good idea or that such a venture could sustain itself. The board was organized, and soon put together a strong inaugural class of eleven inductees, including Bob Lanier, Gil Perreault, and Robert E. Rich Sr., the founder of Rich Products. Since then, each class has been an excellent cross-section of those who have contributed to the rich heritage of sports in Buffalo, and more than two hundred and fifty men and women who lived and worked in Western New York have been honored by the organization at its annual awards banquets.

Today, the *Buffalo News* is a huge backer of the Hall and typically does a series of articles on the inductees. And the dinners are routinely sold out. You can visit the Hall's exhibit in the pavilion area of the First Niagara Center in downtown Buffalo.

Thanks, Kap.

BUFFALO FAMILIES

This section could not possibly accommodate the names of all the families that have greatly impacted the growth and success of commerce and sports in Western New York. But here are a few: the Schoellkopf family in Niagara Falls, the Knox family, the Rich family, the Breuil family, the Wilson family of Detroit, and the Pastor family, whose roots were in Brooklyn. There are many others.

Without them, much of what we take for granted in Western New York would never have come to pass. Jim Breuil's stake in the Bills of the AAFC put the city's name on the list of prospective sites for a professional football team. It got Ralph Wilson's attention, and his faith in the Buffalo community has never wavered. Without it, there would be no Buffalo Bills.

The Sabres, like the Bills, are part of the fabric of Buffalo, and Buffalonians can thank the Knox family for a large part of that legacy and for the downtown hockey arena, the First Niagara

Center. The Knoxes worked tirelessly to put the financing together to make it all possible. I don't know what the deal is for naming rights, but I hope someday it could be called the Knox Arena. It seems only right.

The Pastor family kept professional hockey alive in the AHL long enough for the Knox family to arouse NHL interest. The Rich family has kept pro baseball alive for decades, now in a state-of-the-art facility in downtown Buffalo.

The sports teams in Buffalo form the backbone of the community. But it would be a mistake to ignore the critical role played by the area's outstanding institutes of higher learning, or to fail to note the world of arts and entertainment. The contemporary collection of the Albright-Knox (that name again) Art Gallery ranks among the best in the world, and the Buffalo Philharmonic Orchestra is a treasure, playing in one of the most acoustically perfect music halls in the world. Its list of conductors approaches a who's who in the world of concert music. Theater productions abound. Shea's Performing Arts Center hosts the best of Broadway, and local productions that rival any in the country dot the neighborhoods.

By the way, there are no bad restaurants in Western New York. If one opens, it doesn't last long. Buffalo's contributions to the food world are wildly popular: beef on 'weck, Friday fish fries, and, of course, chicken wings. But beyond these comfort foods, the variety and quality of fine, casual and ethnic eating establishments in Western New York, many featuring world-class chefs, rivals that of any big city I have visited.

CAN'T ROAM FAR FROM THE NEST

The nest in this compilation is the nest in which I lived and worked for many years. Retirement — even to a sunnier climate — no matter how enjoyable, can't sever the umbilical cord that, in my case, as for most Buffalonians, is forever intact.

I get my Buffalo fix first thing in the morning after making coffee by going to that monster known as the computer. It was still a baby when I quit working, but has grown into an addiction. It is a tool for staying in touch and calms the nerves. Believe it or not, I still go to the weather report, then scan the obits in the *Buffalo News*. Next to the sports pages, then the columns. I peruse the home pages of the Sabres, the Bills, and the Bisons, even in the off-season. I look at the UB football team and the scores for the high school hoops teams. I can't help myself, and I have no intention of finding a cure.

I check Channel 7's home page, and a day does not go by without an email exchange with Irv, who's out in California. He's as addicted to staying in touch with Buffalo as I am. Tom's fix is easier; he still lives in Western New York.

Here in Whispering Pines, North Carolina, where I live, I find myself bragging about the food in Buffalo. Thanks to Buffalonians Steve and Liz Pattison, there is a place nearby called Darlings, where they make a fish fry with haddock and know what beef on 'weck is. Salvation. I watch Bills games there every Sunday with several other expatriates. Some Patriots fans gather there, too, but we get along.

At home in Whispering Pines, North Carolina.

Most of what I've written here are simply my reflections, and remembering can be difficult. One thought leads to another and then another, and eventually things come to you that you'd long forgotten. It's a very soul-cleansing exercise. During the process you realize how fortunate you are to have lived the life you've lived, to have come from the family you came from, to have had the family you and your wife created, and to have enjoyed the wonderful experiences that have enriched your life.

There are many bumps and turns along life's path, even in the best of circumstances. Sometimes we are successful in smoothing the bumps and straightening the turns. Sometimes we're not. When Paul Newman played Rocky Graziano in a film about the fighter's life, in the closing scene he says the line that inspired the film's title: "Somebody up there likes me."

I now know what he meant. When events in your life are happening, you mostly just roll with the punches. It's not a time to reflect; it's a time to do your job, in the workplace and at home. My time of reflection has finally arrived and I can't believe how lucky I have been. The realization comes as you tell stories about this person or that event, and you understand that most people never get to experience what you have experienced, or talk to the people with whom you have spoken. But it was my job ... and I loved doing it.

Reflecting on a life in broadcasting... How lucky can a guy get?

ACKNOWLEDGMENTS

The phrase "thank you" isn't enough to fully express my gratitude to all those who encouraged me and assisted with this project — you know who you are. Names like Pat, Chet, Bill.... My wife, Edith, who has been the sounding board for everything that has been written. And those who helped pull the project together in its final stages: Elizabeth Gerhman for her excellent editorial work, David Staba for his insights on sports history, Lynn King for her legal advice, Jon Guevara for his design work, and Marti Gorman of Buffalo Heritage Press for agreeing to take on the project.

In my professional career I'd like to thank the bosses I worked for at Channel 7. Bob King, Larry Pollack, and Phil Beuth encouraged all who worked for them to express themselves and fly with abandon. And the dozens of producers, reporters, cameramen, and studio technicians who seldom, if ever, appeared on television. Without them Irv, Rick, and Tom never would have survived. Thanks also to those who worked with me in the sports department: Bob Koshinski, Brenda Brennan, Anne Simon, Clip Smith, Mark Cooper, Rick Swenson, and Bob Dingwall. I am forever grateful to have known and worked with them.

When I finally succumbed to the urgings of family and friends to write this compendium of recollections, I failed to take into consideration how long it had been since I retired; that 23-year hiatus was a great burden on my fading memory. So, it has been my good fortune to be able to turn to my friend, *Buffalo News* sportswriter Milt Northrop, for advice and direction. I don't know anyone whose memory is so vast and instantaneous, rivaled perhaps only by the legendary pro football reporter Larry Felser, also of the *News*. When I posed the possibility of writing a book, Milt encouraged the venture and kept after me to GET IT DONE. I am indebted to him for his encouragement, his advice, and especially his friendship. The process has reminded me that the transition from reporter to fan is never quite complete; the journalist mantle never fades.

PHOTO: BILL WIPPERT / THE BUFFALO NEWS

Back cover photo: Rick Azar standing in front of the house he lived in during high school and college, formerly 139 Elmwood Avenue in the Allentown neighborhood in Buffalo, NY. Taken by his son, Jeff Carballada, in 2010.

INDEX